DO NOT REMOVE
CARDS FROM POCKET

Rod
Stewart

By
Paul Nelson
& Lester Bangs

Rod Stew

art

Paul Nelson
& Lester Bangs

Delilah Books
Distributed by G.P. Putnam's Sons
NEW YORK

ISBN: *0-933328-08-7*

Library of Congress Catalog Card Number: 81-67648

DELILAH BOOKS
A division of Delilah Communications Ltd.
118 E. 25th St.
New York, N.Y. 10010

MANUFACTURED IN THE UNITED STATES OF AMERICA

Book and cover design by VINCENT AND MARTINE WINTER

SPECIAL THANKS TO:
Sheila Rock, for her invaluable photo research, Ed Caraeff, Wes Goodwin, Virginia Rubel, Keith Korman, Karen Moline, Mercury/Decca Records, Riva Records, all contributing photographers and photo agencies for their patience and marvelous pictures, and Stephanie Peters for her design assistance.

PHOTO CREDITS

RICHARD AARON *p. 35, p. 69 (top), p. 70 (top R), p. 114, p. 115, pp. 118–119, pp. 126–127, p. 143.* MICHAEL BRENNAN/SCOPE FEATURES *p. 146.* LEEE CHILDERS/NEAL PETERS *p. 42, p. 153.* COLLECTION NEAL PETERS *p. 77.* ROBERT ELLIS *p. 157.* DEZO HOFFMAN/REX FEATURES LTD. *p. 51, p. 55, p. 57, p. 68 (bottom), p. 75, p. 79, p. 81, p. 99.* LONDON FEATURES INTL. *p. 67, p. 68 (top), p. 69 (bottom R), p. 72, pp. 102–103.* MARK MACLAREN *p. 120.* JANET MACOSKA/LONDON FEATURES INTL. *p. 48.* PAUL McALPINE *p. 22, p. 41, p. 43, p. 97.* MERCURY/DECCA RECORDS *p. 90, p. 91.* CLAUDE MOUGIN *p. 30, pp. 36–37, p. 47, pp. 114–115 (center), p. 116.* ROBIN PLATZER *p. 40, p. 137.* CHUCK PULIN *p. 34, p. 83, p. 111, p. 131.* REX FEATURES *p. 70 (bottom R), p. 150.* RIVA RECORDS *p. 12, p. 18, p. 19, p. 32, p. 39, p. 45, p. 82, p. 85, p. 88, pp. 92–93, p. 94, p. 100, p. 107, p. 121, p. 125, p. 128, p. 133, p. 139, p. 154.* MICK ROCK *p. 66, p. 68 (bottom L), p. 69 (bottom L), p. 70 (top L), p. 71 (bottom R), p. 73, p. 96.* SCOPE FEATURES *p. 117.* KATE SIMON/TOPIX *p. 71 (bottom L), p. 104, p. 112.* SKR PHOTOS/LONDON FEATURES INTL. *pp. 86–87, p. 147.* DAVID STEEN/SCOPE FEATURES *pp. 8–9, p. 15, pp. 16–17, p. 71 (top R), p. 123, p. 141, pp. 144–145, p. 149.* JOSEPH STEVENS *p. 63, p. 70 (bottom L), p. 71 (top L), p. 108, p. 109, p. 130, p. 148.* TOPIX *p. 27.* CHARLYN ZLOTNICK *p. 25.*

2150030

PREFACE

I have always believed that rock 'n' roll comes down to myth. There are no "facts." When *Rolling Stone* avers it's printing "All the News That Fits," it's not talking about news, it's talking about hype. Which is what the rock press comes down to.

Rod Stewart knows this; that's why all his early bios/profiles are hopelessly confusing—like Dylan and so many others, he deliberately filled them with contradictory fabrications, because he knew that rock 'n' roll is about reinventing yourself, and succeeded brilliantly.

Take this book in that spirit. Some of it is "true"—exhaustively researched, and *most* of those sections involving quotes from previously published materials, especially attributed ones, may be regarded as the "truth." I made up the rest, with the exception of the first chapter, which is a genuine account about two friends, and the "Jewish Mothers" dialogue between Paul and myself, and Paul's record critique sections.

So believe what you choose to; ultimately, it makes no difference. Rod will continue to sell records no matter what happens here. The purpose of this book is not to sell records: it is to entertain—and never the twain shall meet. And to play with the myth of Rod Stewart, as built up over all these years.

Enjoy. I did.

LESTER BANGS

June 28, 1981

On Tour 1977-78

CHAPTER I

That's no' just a game of football played by professionals, that's you on trial for your life. And they wonder why everybody drinks at these games? I'll tell you why, your guts are churning so bad you need to be half-bevvied or you'd faint. Please God let us win this year. Please God don't let the team do anything silly. Please God give Scotland a break.
—IAN ARCHER AND TREVOR ROYLE,
We'll Support Evermore, a book about Scottish football

*Now you ask me if I'm sincere
That's the question that I always fear
Verse seven was never clear...*
—ROD STEWART,
"I Was Only Joking"

I.   San Antonio

ROD STEWART'S HOTEL ROOM IS ONE VAST PILE OF DANCER'S TIGHTS, BODY STOCKINGS and ballet slippers. Not any ordinary tights, stocking and slippers, mind you, but the finest that finance can finagle: apparel so expensive and expansive that I think for a

9

moment about Daisy weeping over a stack of Gatsby's luxurious shirts. Then I have to laugh out loud.

There seems to have been a fire storm of pastels in here, and the effect is incredible: a veritable montage of money. It's as if Capezio had exploded, spraying every square foot of the suite with shrapnel so chic it could only inflict the so-called "million-dollar wound." Servants sort through the royal rubble looking for Cinderella's slipper. Another trunk is opened, and the air is filled with flying silks and soft pigskin. An aquamarine ballet shoe lands in my lap. "Hot Legs," a song from the recent *Foot Loose & Fancy Free*, pounds away on a huge cassette machine, while Tony Toon, Stewart's personal assistant, calls the star "she." Is this the true story of rock & roll?

In dilettantish disarray, Stewart himself is striding through the debris like some suave, henna-headed Hamlet, soliloquizing about the problem of having two blue slippers for his left foot, none for his right. He's serious, but he's not serious. Somehow, he still looks like a football player, and I'm glad. He seems to be thinking about a dozen things at once, telling me about a Scottish flag he's got hanging out one of his windows, talking about an old Bob Dylan tune he'd like to record, and remembering our days together at Mercury Records. We're good friends, and it feels that way, but we're both more than a little nervous about the formal circumstances of this meeting.

I just can't imagine doing a hatchet job on you, I tell him, praying to myself he hasn't changed much. "You're in My Heart," "You Got a Nerve" and "I was Only Joking" sound like the same old Rod to me.

He's apparently never heard the phrase *hatchet job* before, and it makes him smile. He repeats it a few times, then tells me about a bad review from Miami. The temperature rises. "I appreciate what you say," he says. Someone hands him a blue slipper. "But, at the same time, I hope you'll write what you see." It's for his right foot.

We seem to have made a separate peace.

IN THE ELEVATOR going down to the lobby, Stewart remembers I once asked him why "Tonight's the Night" was his only happy love song. "I was so surprised," he says. "Then I realized that what you said was *true*."

One of the roadies pipes up: "They all ought to be happy!"

"Noooooooo," Rod wails, slapping palm to forehead. His face contorts into an expression of ersatz anguish, and he falls straight backward into the wall.

The whole band cracks up laughing.

On the way to the concert, the limo is ordered to slow down as we all cheer the Scottish flag hanging from the eleventh floor of the Hilton Palacio del Rio.

IN THE DRESSING ROOM, we get a chance to talk a bit. An English couple has sent Stewart a bottle of John Courage beer. There's a note tied to a Tartan scarf around the bottle's neck. They've driven several hundred miles and want to come backstage. Rod tries to arrange it.

He says he and the band are getting their second wind now, revving up for the December dates at the Forum in Los Angeles. That this new band—Jim Cregan, Gary Grainger, Billy Peek (guitars), John Jarvis (keyboards), Phil Chen (bass), Carmine Appice (drums)—is one with which he'll "make a last stand, unless we become complacent." It's clear that Stewart regards his final days with his former group, the Faces, as nothing more than "parody."

When he talks about Los Angeles, he often makes that city sound like some youthful prairie town dreamed of and longed for by the aging heroine of a Willa Cather

10

novel. It's not Scotland, he admits, and he misses London, but to him the Forum concerts signify the triumphant return of a "local lad," whereas he always feels "inadequate" and like an "outsider" in the East, especially in New York City. "No matter how many times I've played it," he says, "there's still something about Madison Square Garden that terrifies me."

Stewart would seem to be a man who needs communal roots: the camaraderie of a rock & roll band, a friendly city to call his own. "These fucking people who criticize Hollywood," he says. "They've never even lived there. They're a million miles on the other side of the world, and they think that bloody Garbos and people like that still walk around the streets. Really, I think it's a fine rock & roll city. It's a little bit sleepy—it's not as fast as New York—but it's good enough for me to come back to for three or four months, and I won't have anybody knocking it. I mean, I love the place."

"Hot Legs" blasts from the cassette machine as the band tries to tune. I'm starting to think how much fun it is being on a rock & roll tour again. Rod looks at his "boys," many of them unknowns, with a father's pride, and I almost expect him to give me a cigar. Instead, he says: "Tonight may not be so good because the acoustics are terrible here. But wait till Denver. We'll really be hot then."

AFTER THE CONCERT—which was, as predicted, mediocre—fifteen or twenty of Stewart's congregation gather for a big supper in the hotel's swank river-level restaurant. It's like *Monty Python's Flying Circus*, directed by John Ford. Voices are raised in beery, maudlin song, and there's a wonderful scene in which everybody toasts the road manager and his shy young lady by singing "Falling in Love Again" every few minutes or so, with Rod providing a letter-perfect imitation of Marlene Dietrich. He also launches into a very soulful rendition of "I Don't Want to Talk About It," only to have the song punctuated, in mock-military manner, by the whole crew shouting "Sah!" after each repetition of the title line. Everybody tells lots of stories and jokes, most of them corny when taken down verbatim, all of them quite touching in the context of comradeship. The code of the road is at work again. Clearly, this is a group of people with no serious ego problems.

A long procession of prospective groupies wanders in and out. One has braids and a big chest. Stewart signs a blouse, the leather patch on the ass of someone's blue jeans, and a soccer ball. Billy Peek, who is very quiet, is approached by a girl who talks so slowly that it takes her forever to get past the two *l*s in his first name: "Bi*llll*...*lllly*." He doesn't seem interested. Some of us try to think up new dialogue for movies like *The Big Sleep* and *Casablanca*. Sample: "Do you want to fool around?" "We wouldn't be fooling, would we?"

Rod disappears, so I walk over to the Alamo. It looks just like I thought it would: a white, Spanish-style building, front-lit, under a clear Texas sky, half-moon rising. At three in the morning, there's no traffic. The streets are absolutely empty. The plaque on the door reads:

> *Be silent, friend*
> *Here heroes died*
> *To blaze a trail*
> *For other men.*

I sit for a while on a bench by a phone booth in front of the Alamo. Just thinking.

11

Wishing I knew who to call. Moved once again by heroic history. For some reason, I write down the number of the pay phone: (512) 223-0084.

TONIGHT, SAN ANTONIO looks more like Paris or Venice than Texas. It's a place pictured in fine dreams. There's a canal from some romantic film, bordered by tall trees hung with Christmas lights, running through the center of the city. Along the canal are balconies, bridges, bookstores, small cafes and a lovely Riverwalk (*Paseo del Rio*), now nearly deserted.

As I near the hotel, I notice a man and a woman seated on a white archway that spans the canal. They're talking intently. The man is wearing light tan pants, sporty

12

tan shoes and a leather jacket. The woman seems mesmerized. Christ, right out of *The Way We Were, Blume in Love* or *Obsession,* I remember thinking: Redford and Streisand, Segal and Anspach, Robertson and Bujold. Then I realize it's Stewart and one of the waitresses from the restaurant.

Later, from the lobby, I watch them drive away in a battered pickup with Texas license plates. There are still quite a few fans waiting for autographs and et ceteras. One of them asks if I've seen Rod. I shake my head no. Like the song says, "The crowd don't understand."

II. *Denver*

BRITT EKLAND AND THE SEX PISTOLS ARE INDEED UBIQUITOUS. IF YOU DON'T BELIEVE me, ask Rod Stewart. He can't even walk into a room these days without being buttonholed by journalists who want his opinion about one or the other, and I sense he's getting sick of it. He wants to talk about the success of his latest album, the ongoing tour or his new band—cruelly dubbed the Faceless by certain critics—but nobody cares. Instead, he's constantly quizzed about either the wrath of the wraithlike actress/ex-housemate who's suing him because he left her, or the pugnacity of the punks, who see him as the prototype of the rich, empty rock & roll star—as nothing, really nothing, to turn off. Britt wants his money (and, out of court, recently settled for a chunk of it), while the Pistols and their fans don't want his art. To a lot of people, it's as simple as that. Beauty and the beasts must be driving this man crazy.

In a way, they are. Whenever I mention Ekland, Stewart seems to wish I were someplace else. He rolls his eyes like some sulky Sisyphus contemplating the inevitability of the hill and the rock. He's not pleased with questions about Johnny Rotten either, though he tries hard not to be overly negative about Britain's New Wave musical scene. (His two favorites: the Stranglers and Graham Parker and the Rumour.) But what really galls Rod, I think, is the change in attitude of a number of key critics toward him. Ever since the Sex Pistols cast the first stone, too many boulders have followed.

• John Rockwell in *The New York Times:* "In person, Mr. Stewart comes close to defining the word 'vulgarity.' He dresses in a manner that can only be called silly, tarting himself up in androgynous glitter and assuming all kinds of transparently artificial melodramatic poses. Mr. Stewart is the sort of rocker who can take on the trappings of Las Vegas and not be suspected of selling out, because a Vegas notion of glamor seems to have been his inner ideal all along.... He remains a lesser artist than the real greats of rock."

• Joe McEwen in *Rolling Stone:* "There are a lot of kids in England who don't care what kind of fashionably gauche trinkets decorate Rod Stewart's high-class Hollywood home or what the exact terms (if any) of his separation from Britt Ekland will be. They do care that Stewart has lost touch with them, not only musically but culturally as well.... As for *Foot Loose & Fancy Free,* it's sure hard to care much about 'Hot Legs' with Elvis Costello and the Sex Pistols around."

While Stewart has enough confidence to think he's at the apex of his art, he's too smart not to be worried, though he's tight-lipped about it. Ironically, now that he's become somewhat of a workaholic (the band toured or made records nine of the last twelve months) and very serious about his career, he's considered more of a playboy than ever. While it's clear that everyone who's traveling with him loves him because he genuinely seems to be just one of the boys, it's also apparent that much of the world no longer shares that opinion.

Me? I'm still a believer, but then I like the guy. Maybe he's lost a little of his personal self-awareness, yet his songs remain sharp, and I trust the emotions behind those songs. Granted, Rod could never have written either "Anarchy in the U.K." or "God Save the Queen." Is Johnny Rotten capable of the warmth and wisdom of "You're in My Heart"?

THE STEWART ENTOURAGE travels in a Viscount four-engine turbo jet done out in three rooms. In the center room, Rod and a Scottish sound mixer (who's had two double Screwdrivers for breakfast and speaks in an accent so thick it's a good thing we're not flying through it) immediately put on a video cassette of a football match. It's England versus Scotland—Rough and McGrain are two of the Scottish players, I note—and there's lots of beer and shouting on the plane as well as in the stadium. Things get so bleary and rowdy that when Scotland's team scores a goal, everybody misses seeing it, and Stewart has to rewind the tape. "It only happened two years ago," he says, winking in my direction.

Carmine Appice on English football: "If you get bored, the American section's up here."

IN THE DENVER HILTON, Rod Stewart puts his hands and nose into fresh cement for posterity. The local Peaches record store came up with the idea, but since Tony Toon isn't sure he can get Stewart down there, the store brings the sidewalk to Stewart. Two workmen carry it in. Rod performs with his hands first, then improvises the climax. His sense of humor and uncanny knack for making the right remark at precisely the right time have rarely been better. As he puts towel to forehead and presses his infamous beak into the wet cement, he asks, with a great deal of concern: "Are there any people on the floor below?"

STEWART, TOON, JIM Cregan, Doris Tyler, Rita Taggart and I are driven to a Denver discotheque/steakhouse for a late supper. Tyler (in charge of costumes and makeup) and Taggart (an actress and the tour masseuse) are called, with no accuracy and great respect, the Vibrator Sisters. They're two of the smartest, funniest ladies living, and Rod loves to have them around. "I'm glad you like them," he tells me later. "Everyone else on the tour can get so serious, but they're always like the spirit of rock & roll."

In the restaurant, people constantly ask for the star's autograph. His meal is interrupted several times, but he seems amazingly unconcerned about it. "What price glory?" Rita whispers to me as a blue-haired matron from the next table leans over to introduce her husband—who doesn't really react—to Rod. Stewart just smiles at him and says: "I can see you're not impressed. Can't say that I blame you."

Rod and Jim start talking about their parents, who still live in England. In a matter of minutes, they're off on a familial marathon, running the gamut from awesome sentiment and awful sentimentality. The stories are wonderful to hear. Stewart thinks so much of his mother and father he even makes recordings of reunions of the clan, claiming he gets most of his best lines that way: "I look to me family for a sense of humor. When I go back to them, they truly make me laugh, though I don't know if I'm laughing at them or with them. Either way, I want to be with them." Though the restaurant is very noisy, I turned on the cassette machine. Rod is saying:

14

*R*od at home, reviewing his prized collection of the complete works of Edgar G. Ulmer.

"Me and me dad were going to a football match, and me dad came out in his old coat—and it was *rough*. It was an old black coat and he had outgrown it, and me mum said: "*You* can't go out in that bloody old coat! Your son's a millionaire. You'll disgrace the street.' Funny.

"Then there was this thing about the wine, because no one drinks wine at me house, right? But I brought a bottle of wine in when I was back last time. I opened it up and I said, 'Mum, we have to decanter the wine,' and she said, 'What?' I said: 'We have to decanter. We have to pour it into a decanter.' She said, 'Well, what's that?' I said, 'It's like a big vase,' and she said, 'We'll take the flowers out of the vase on top of the television and put it in there.' I said, 'No, we can't do that,' and

18

she said: 'Oh, there's an empty milk bottle outside. Why don't you put the wine in the milk bottle?' Little things like that really bring you back to square one. Me mum's a classic.

"Three years ago, we had a gathering of the clan. I hired three bagpipers in full regalia for New Year's Eve. Just as the clock struck twelve, they came in and played 'Amazing Grace.' You know how 'Amazing Grace' goes. On the pipes, it's so stirring. Me dad cried his eyes out. I'll never forget it. The only thing that could bring a tear to me dad's eye was the sound of pipes and when Scotland scored a goal. Especially against England.

"Ron Wood, he talks about his dad like he was a fucking hero. When the Faces started to make a lot of money, he bought his dad a color television. And his dad was so proud of his color television that he had it chained to the wall, in case somebody tried to steal it. To this day....

"Me and me dad were at a football match at Wembley. It was halftime, and I went downstairs to get a drink. When I came up, me dad was crying. I said, 'What are you crying for?' He said, 'You should have seen it.' The whole fucking Wembley—80,000 Scots—were all singing 'Sailing.' And me dad thinks, 'Me boy started all that.' That means more to me than anything.''

BACK AT THE HOTEL, Rod and I sit down and tape an interview for about two-and-a-half hours. It doesn't go very well, and we both know it. Stewart invites Cregan to stick around, apparently so we can't delve into anything too deeply. At the same

19

time, he's sympathetic toward the problems of my job. I get the feeling he wants to get this thing out of the way quickly, with as much dignity as possible for both of us. He answers everything honestly— sometimes too honestly, I think—but his heart's just not in it.

Stewart on the new band: "Musically, this band is totally superior. I always feel that what we sound like onstage is what the Faces were always trying to sound like —a tightly knit rhythm section with a piano and a lot of rhythm guitar on top of that. The Faces never had it, but there's something the Faces had that this band will never have. I mean, the thing with me and Woody together."

On being criticized by the British punk bands: "What the fuck! I make records. You don't have to buy them if you don't want them. Shit, leave them alone. What am I supposed to do with the money I earn? Give it back? Give it away?

"As Pete Townshend said on television the other week: 'I've made my mark. I've done the records. It's up to them to come and knock me off the top position.' That's the way it should be, but I wouldn't have had the guts to say that. I love him for doing it. I think that fucking guy's magic. He's done it all. He's served his fucking dues. These cunts haven't.

"They say, Well, fucking Rod's gone to Hollywood with a movie star, right? The cunts! I come from the same background as they do. In England, all rock & roll comes from the working class. That's your only way of getting out of the rabble. I come from nothing. Then, all of a sudden, I'm faced with a lot of glamorous women. What the fuck am I going to do?

"The Sex Pistols have a big album now. A lot of money's being grossed. A couple of million dollars. And they'll get paid for it. Then we'll see what they do. Give it back to the fucking record buyers? That's anarchy, isn't it?

"The whole New Wave has destroyed itself immediately. A second and third wave will come from there. The summer before last, it looked promising. Then the big fucking record companies came in, the big fucking business moguls. All of a sudden, there were clothes designers and punk fashion shows. That's what killed it for me. It's really dead in England. The first wave's dead.

"In America [with the New York Dolls, et al.], it was a music period. In England, it's a fashion foremost, an attitude, a stance. Which isn't the way it should be. It's phony bollocks. So let's wait for the second wave. That might bring on something good."

On *Foot Loose & Fancy Free*: "It was supposed to be a double album, but we had to stop because of the tour. There was no concept. A lot of the tracks reflect what I was going through at the time with Britt. In fact, I knew the title of the album before we busted up. It must have been in the back of me mind that it was going to happen. The title is a straightforward statement of independence. I felt I'd been tied down for too long and I wanted to break away. Domesticity—that's death for me."

On "You Got a Nerve": "Sometimes what you're writing about is what you *wouldn't* want to happen to you. I couldn't think of anything worse than that—the woman goes off and she fucks somebody else on the other side of the world and comes back and says, 'Let me in.' I've never been mistreated like that. Perhaps I'm asking for it. It hasn't happened yet, and I wouldn't wish it on my worst enemies. People say to me, 'This must be about Britt. She's done that to you.' And I say, no, she hasn't done that to me. She had no bearing on the song whatsoever."

On "(If Loving You Is Wrong) I Don't Want to Be Right": "That really fit into what was happening. I was seeing Liz Treadwell, but Britt didn't know. The whole

20

track was done live in the studio. Liz was there, and I'm singing, 'If loving you is wrong, I don't want to be right....' You couldn't *help* but sing it with guts. That was the last track we recorded."

On "You're in My Heart (the Final Acclaim)": "It wasn't totally about Britt. The first verse could have been about Liz. It could have been about anybody that I met in that period—and there were a lot of them. It's about three women, two football teams and a country—Scotland."

On the line, "You'll be my breath should I grow old": "I think that must have been about me mum and dad."

BEFORE THE SOUNDCHECK the next afternoon, Stewart is sitting on the edge of the stage, playing Woody Guthrie songs on an acoustic guitar. He looks at the myriad of roadies setting up the band's equipment. "Shit, there are people on this tour I don't even know yet," he says sadly.

I like soundchecks. You can sit way in the back of an empty auditorium and think —if I only knew what to think. Something about all that open space just gets the mind rolling, and it's such a contrast to the pandemonium of the show later. During the soundcheck, the band is perfectly relaxed, and the playing always seems to have that something extra—naturalness, I suppose—that invariably strikes me as being more private and revealing (i.e., better) than the official version. I think someone should start making live soundcheck LPs.

I'm totally schizophrenic about Stewart and his new band in concert. From a distance, everything appears overwrought and impersonal: Rod playing straight through to the audience with the broadest possible star appeal, the meaning of the songs be damned. But up closer, where I can see his face, he looks like a man who's completely sincere. And his interpretations not only make sense, they're very moving.

I can't really figure it out.

III.   *Los Angeles*

JIM CREGAN SEEMS TO HAVE TAKEN RON WOOD'S PLACE AS ROD STEWART'S number-one road buddy. They're together most of the time. Cregan, Rod confides—in a tone so reverent it's ridiculous—is the only reason he doesn't allow tickets to be sold for the seats behind the stage. That way, Jim's bald spot won't show.

In return, Cregan tells a lovely story about how Stewart recorded the highly confessional "I Was Only Joking." The first time any of the musicians heard the lyrics was during the vocal take, since Rod had simply scat sung or hummed in the appropriate places while the instrumental tracks were cut. When he finally sang the words, he did it rather sheepishly, shyly glancing up at the band every few seconds to see if they thought the song was too corny. They didn't.

STEWART AND I are sitting in his home, talking about the old days, watching yet another video cassette of Scottish football and seeking to discover whether either of us has improved his technique in the art of the formal interview. "So it's come to this," he says, and we both laugh. I ask him how he's suddenly become such a prolific songwriter.

"I think I spoke to Bernie [Taupin] once," he says. "I asked him how he and Elton [John] went about writing songs. And he said: 'Well, I write the lyrics, I give them to Elton, and he just sits down at the piano and makes with the music. It's as

easy as that.' I thought, shit, me and Woody don't work like that. It's really hard work when we do it because we do it the other way around. There's no freedom in doing it our way. You're stuck—you've got to make each word fit the music.'' He shakes his head in disbelief. ''So, after years and years, I suddenly learned how to write songs.''

Out of the blue, Rod admits: ''I want to see how good the band is. I keep shouting me mouth off about them, but I want to *really* see how good they are. I want to get away from the way we are now. Perhaps I shouldn't say this, but we're not really gaining any new ground. We're doing something now that I love—making good rock & roll—but I think there's a lot more to rock & roll. We're going to try to start taking it away from the Chuck Berry rhythm guitar and the regular chords.''

22

Does Stewart think he and Britt Ekland will ever get back together?

"Well, it's impossible at the moment. We aren't going to get back together. I look upon it probably as being a big mistake. It might be a mistake on my behalf, it could have been a mistake on her behalf. I know we were good for each other. Very good for each other. Who made the first bad move, whether it was because of what I did or because of her reaction to what I did, I don't know. All I know is what I did was legal."

Legal?

"What I did was not breaking any law whatsoever. There was never a pact between us. I think perhaps in a drunken moment, I might have said I'd try to be faithful, but she knew me track record when she met me. And I did me best but I fell short, like many of us do. I'm still a sucker for a pretty face and a pair of long legs, but I'm the only fuck-poor bastard who's ever got sued over it.

"It's difficult to know what to say because everything I say nowadays seems to get completely blown out of proportion and thrown back in me face. Just for the record, I'm totally fucking fed up with reading about meself, especially in the European press. So I'm very reluctant to talk about it. But she's nowhere near as bad as people make out she is. I mean, she's the most dedicated woman I've ever known when it comes to being with one guy, and I appreciate that. Her biggest problem is there's always been a language barrier there. A lot of people didn't ever understand her. She doesn't speak the Queen's English, and I think that many times when she'd try to be funny, it came across as being cynical and sarcastic.

"But the fucking amount of money [$12.5 million] she's trying to sue me for! There isn't that much money in the world, I'm sure. I make nowhere near that much. But I think when a woman's been hurt like I hurt her—because I completely crushed her world around her—they just become irrational and do the most wicked thing. She always did say she'd cut me balls off, but I didn't know what she meant. Now I know what she meant. She didn't *literally* mean she'd cut me balls off. She'd cut me wallet off."

(In her book, *True Britt*, Ekland remembers it this way: "Once Rod told me that his other women hadn't cared if he slept around. I looked at him straight between the eyes. 'Then that's where I'm very different,' I said. 'I would mind a great deal. In fact, if you screw another woman while you're with me, I'll chop off your balls.' Rod's face puckered with fear. He knew that I meant every word.")

What would Stewart have done if the tables had been turned?

"She knows that. I told her that. I said, 'If you'd have done that to me, you wouldn't have heard anything. That would have been it.' I'd have been off or she'd have been kicked out of me house—there would have been no coming back. It's never happened to me, thank God, as far as I know, and I'm pretty sure I'm shrewd enough that I'd know if it ever did. That would be it. I'd say goodbye. I mean, if I can't give a woman everything, then fuck it."

I find it difficult to believe his claim that he's never been hurt in love.

"Never. I've always been the one to push and shove and say, Sorry, that's it, darlin', it's all over, goodbye. Take twenty Valiums and have a stomach pump and that's the end of it. I've been very lucky, but I know that one day I'm going to get fucking stung something terrible."

I still wonder why he did it.

"Boys will be boys, Paul," he says with a sigh of resignation. He's not smiling.

STEWART AND I once played a game of pool in Miami Beach. I beat him, and he's never forgotten it. Of course, I haven't let him. Now he wants his revenge. He builds up a strong early lead, but I distract him by asking questions. (He kept bumping my arm every time I was about to shoot in Florida.) I mention something about "You're in My Heart."

He says: "A few days ago in San Antonio, I woke up with that bird. Woke up, and the old sun was coming through the curtains. She says to me, 'Go and turn the radio on.' Out comes: 'I didn't know what day it was....' There's fucking magic in it! It wasn't the lyrical content. It was just, shit, that's my song that I wrote when I was in bed at home and I had the flu. And here I am in the middle of San Antonio with a strange woman about a million miles from me hotel, and here it comes on the radio. I think it's the most marvelous thing in the world. Your song goes through the channels, it's pressed, it's a bit of plastic and it comes all the way back to you. And there's your feelings, coming through a radio. Does that sound really silly?"

I tell him I don't think so.

"I mean, there's this fucking thing where no one seems to grow old," he says. "You might get a few wrinkles around your eyes, but the instinct is still there. It's there in front of us all the time. All of these women. And if it's flashed in front of your face, you want to take it. Who wouldn't?

"It's like we're in a time capsule. Without flattering meself, I know I look exactly the same as I did seven years ago. It's not that you're not allowed to grow older, it's just that time goes so quickly that you haven't got time to grow older—in attitude, appearance or anything. It's almost like we're not growing up at all.

"Sometimes I look at meself and I think, fuck, you're the same person with the same basic needs as you were five years ago. And that shouldn't be. I'm thirty-two now and I think, shit, I must be a bit more mature. But I'm not. Still gullible for a long leg and a big tit." He can't help but smile. "I always look upon meself as being very immature."

(Ekland in *True Britt*: "He was still a boy, not a man.")

Rod starts talking about his collection of *objets d'art* while I put together a four-ball run.

"I'm sure everybody must think I spend every day standing on the terrace watching the fucking football matches," he says. "But, of course, I don't. I want to spend the money that I'm earning. I go off to Paris and buy lamps and things like that.

"The first thing I ever bought of any price was a sterling silver picture frame that I bought with the first week's royalties I ever got from Jeff Beck. I just saw it in the store, and it was a beautiful thing. I've still got it.

"No one's ever collected in me family. I supppose I was just trying to improve meself. It might have been that. It might have just been the fact that whatever I started collecting was so interesting, so beautiful. I've always admired beauty in anything, whether it be a painting, motor cars, the way someone plays football, the way they sing, or whether it's a lamp. I think that's one thing you don't *learn*. You certainly can't learn that."

Is there any one thing he particularly wants?

"Oh, yeah, hundreds. Hundreds. But if there's one thing I'd love to have, it would be a painting by J.M.W. Turner. But no one's got that much money. I don't even know as there's ever been one up for sale. But, more than that, I want Scotland to win the World Cup. There's a book—"

Stewart brings out a copy of *We'll Support Evermore* and reads aloud the quote that begins this chapter. When I write it down in my notebook, he's very concerned that

I get it right. It clearly means a lot to him.

"That sort of sums it up," he says. Then he decides otherwise. "No, it doesn't. You never sum up anything."

I sink the eight ball into the corner pocket. Rod looks extremely pained. Much as I like the guy, he sure can't shoot pool. But then, there's a lot of things I can't do either.

PAUL NELSON

25

Two Jewish Mothers

Pose As Rock Critics

CHAPTER II

LESTER: WHERE DO YOU THINK WOULD BE A GOOD PLACE TO BEGIN WITH THIS?

PAUL: The general position that we think he's in?

Yeah. You start, because you're the expert here. Or at least less of an unbeliever at this point than I am.

Well, I think he's a really complex guy. Yet the last time I talked to him, or it seems like every time I've seen him, there's been a little less of him that I could relate to. Each time I talked to him he seemed less and less aware of what the whole outer world was, and more and more closed off from it, because of management and—

What did it seem like he was really interested in? Or could you tell?

Nothing much. I mean other than his world seemed to consist of him. Basically he was pissed off because they were putting out ballads as singles and he was a rock 'n' roller. We were watching some video of his new ad at his house and he was going on, ranting and raving about how this wasn't right and that wasn't right. And from the whole conversation we had had about punk rock it seemed to me that he missed completely what was good about it and the point of what they were saying about him. His favorite punk people were Graham Parker who isn't even punk, and the Stranglers who are about the worst imaginable punk band. He was saying, "What the hell do

27

they want me to do with my money? If they want me to give it back ...'' I didn't think that was the point. They weren't attacking him for being rich, it was that he had cut himself off and didn't have anything in common with them or his audience. And he *doesn't* have anything in common—I don't think his audience could reach him anymore.

But isn't that hard for somebody who's in a position like he is; you reach a point where that kind of isolation is inevitable?

It doesn't happen with Springsteen.

Can Bruce Springsteen walk down the street and talk to kids and be a normal person? 'Cause that's not the impression I get.

Well, I think he tries.

Isn't it the nature of the system that it just builds these walls around these people? What was that quote from Elton John a few years back? It was in a magazine article, and he was talking to Johnny Ramone and he said, "You'll see—somehow it just all grows up around you. Turn around one day and there's the limousines and ..."

Yeah, I think he's wanted it that way, I don't think he's tried to fight it. He gets off on it in a way.

Well, it is very seductive.

Probably. I've been backstage at Springsteen shows where Bruce'll open the doors and let the thirty kids hanging around outside come in and talk to him. Hope Antman (CBS Records) told me a story that when Bruce was in Minneapolis and had a night off he went to a movie by himself and this kid recognized him as he was buying a ticket and said ''Hey, you wanna sit with me?'' and he sat with him, and the kid said, ''Hey, you wanna come home and talk and my mother'll fix us some things,'' and Bruce went home with the kid, and spent the whole night with the kid, and that ain't ever gonna happen with Rod Stewart. He's gonna be surrounded by so many limousines and ... Sometimes you get the feeling that he misses it and other times it seems like he's just—

Well, why do you think he's so caught up in that? Do you think it's just a natural or even an inevitable product of growing up poor in the English class system?

Somewhat, perhaps. We might have misinterpreted some of the songs or some of the motives. Maybe it is from growing up as he did, maybe his real goal was to become famous and become a Hollywood starlet. Which, y'know, none of us thought was true; all of us thought he was just the everyday rock 'n' roller, or as close as you could get at that time. Maybe he never really wanted to be that. Maybe he always wanted to hobnob with the rich. But ... he wasn't *poor*, he grew up lower middle-class. He was never dirt-poor.

One thing I've noticed a lot among people around New York who don't really have it yet, is that they actually think that when they become this ideal of the rich famous rock superstar that's going to solve all their problems and they won't have to deal with themselves and their little neuroses, that all that will be a clean slate.

Yeah, but I don't think Rod thinks he has any problems.

He doesn't look very happy.

28

But on the other hand, a movie star isn't expected to write his own dialogue. In Rod Stewart's case, I've always felt that here was a person of enormous talent and sensitivity, but it was sad and inevitable that the more successful he got, the farther he would be removed from the people and places and situations from which he'd drawn for his best songs.

Yeah, that's true—

It's like You Can't Go Home Again.

—but I don't know that he wants to. Or if he does want to I'm not sure that he's aware of it. He goes home in the extent that he's still very close to his parents. He talked very very movingly about them.

But can he write about that?

He hasn't really, no.

It seems that the songs on the last few albums are all about nothing, or they're kinda pathetic attempts to shore up his image as a ladies' man.

Well, somewhere along the line he's gotten—and I read a quote somewhere where he said he *likes* it—this kind of Jayne Mansfield image: a really trashy, not even movie *star* image, but movie *starlet* image; a sort of a male tart. And he apparently likes this.

Why do you think that is?

I have no idea.

Because Jagger sort of does the same thing, but—

Yeah, but he does it more with a sense of humor, where Rod does it with a straight shot of narcissism. With Jagger you get the feeling that there might be another idea behind it that may be a little deeper or may put a spin on it or something, but with Rod it's almost like ''God, here I am, Jayne Mansfield, and you're supposed to be turned on by looking at me.'' I don't think it goes much deeper than that.

When he was on Midnight Special *doing "Passion"*—

I didn't see it.

It was really sad—

I think ''Passion'' is a fairly decent song.

Yeah, it is, and the thing that was saddest about it was you could tell he was really trying and really feeling it, and it still didn't make any difference. It was hard to put your finger on why, except I guess that he was so obviously trying, reaching for the idea, instead of being passionate or in any way embodying the concept.

Well, I think ''Passion''—and I'm sure he's aware of it—is a really revealing song. There's a duality about it: that if you fall in love you're never out of danger, that being with somebody is really dangerous, and the passion is like taking a fall with somebody—

It's hit and run. Certainly his image and things like "D'Ya Think I'm Sexy" fit right in with the singles bar culture, the way a lot of people are now, and how they wanna present themselves. I was standing in line at the bank one day when Rod had just played here, and I heard two guys in the line ahead of me talking about him ("Did you see Rod Stewart?") with real excitement. What he was trying to put across, that very thing we're talking about—they were eating it right up; the very thing that to us might look pathetic looks different to other people. I guess the question is, do they perceive the patheticness? And obviously they don't.

I don't think so, no.

Of course, that's two men talking.

With those costume changes, ballet slippers, this whole Heathcliff-on-the-moors semi-gay routine that he does ... the last time I saw him, the way he was prancing around the stage with all this stuff rendered all the songs practically ludicrous. I think he was trying, in his mind, to present a legitimate rock spectacle, but the songs went right over everybody's head for that spectacle. When I was on tour with him, sometimes I'd sit way in the back and sometimes I'd go right up on stage, and the further back you were the more ridiculous it was—it looked totally insincere. And the closer up you got, it made some sort of sense; the performances weren't really so bad when you could watch his face. Rod was really trying and it was—sometimes—working, but you had to be *so close* to him to tell ... it was very odd. I had mixed emotions about it.

I think that when people put out this hypernarcissistic image, they see to it that there is absolutely no component of vulnerability about it, and yet the vulnerability was always something appealing about Rod going back to the very beginning.

It's pretty hard to fuse the image of the poor boy looking for love along the English Canal with the Jayne Mansfield ''D'Ya Think I'm Sexy''—those are pretty hard images to coalesce and pull off, and so I thought the images cancelled each other out. And lately the poor boy/canal songs have been rather pathetic.

Not just that, but there was also always that kind of self-effacing element. Combined with his getting older, and all the glitzy stuff. He's sort of without defenses now; he's obliged, when it becomes apparent, with reviews, for example, to become hostile.

I think he's genuinely hurt, and doesn't understand why people are coming down on him. I doubt that he has the faintest idea. He said, ''I like to buy antiques, is there anything wrong with that?'' No, there's nothing wrong with that. It's not a crime to be rich, and to like things. He bought a picture frame with the first check he got from Jeff Beck. It really was touching. I don't think that's why people are after him. It's the sexism, and the narcissism and the complete cutoff from everything.

But the sexism and narcissism and misogyny were all there when he did "Stay With Me," and not nearly as many people were complaining.

There was more of a sense of humor about it then.

It was still pretty nasty. It was probably nastier then than it is now, in fact.

Yeah, yeah, but ... he didn't really look like a sort of Playmate calendar then, wasn't shoving himself at you as such a sex object, or at least if he was there was a little humor in it. Whereas now it's almost like steel girders manufactured along the assembly line.

At the same time, in the more recent material you get a feeling you never had before of almost sour grapes, like in "I Was Only Joking": The crowd don't understand. All of a sudden the self-effacement turns to a big melodramatic Hamlet pose—

No, actually I like the song. I asked him about that line; he didn't know what it meant, said it seemed right to put in. He doesn't seem able to talk about his songs at all, or won't. Probably it's because he is basically an intuitive writer, and I don't think he really knew why he put that line in. For me it spoils the song—

Sure it does.

Until then it's been great.

So many artists don't know what their best and worst stuff is, or they'll write something and never even really know what they're trying to get across until later. And when they realize, it can either be, "Gee, I said that? Wonderful!" or "Oh, no! Uh, oh ..."

Yeah, I know ... for me *Blondes Have More Fun* was the only album where absolutely everything fell flat. On *Foolish Behavior* "Oh God, I Wish I Was Home Again" is really terrific, but then there are attempts to go back and recapture earlier themes that are really awful and insincere.

The first time I noticed it was in "The Tradewinds of Our Time." All of a sudden he's heavy and portentous, and wanted to make a big Statement. "You Wear It Well" is a statement that's universal; anybody anywhere could relate to it, but it's not advertising itself. With "The Tradewinds of Our Time"—the very title is embarrassing. It's kitsch.

But it's the kind of kitsch that takes him out of rock and puts him in that netherworld where Elton John and Dolly Parton and all those people are, which is very very popular, but not necessarily to a rock audience—it's like the Grammies. Pretty soon Rod Stewart will be the ideal Grammy winner, y'know. Which I think he'd hate.

It's almost like Dylan on that Budokan tour—"Thankyou, thankyou, ladies and gentlemen,"—all that phony showbiz Las Vegas stuff. They seem to get sort of lost, although Dylan seems more cynical, although maybe he's really just truly out of his mind—

I think he's just sort of lost; I think probably Rod is sort of too, although you've gotta find new subjects somehow and where he is now they're pretty hard to find. What are you gonna write about, your business manager?

That's what seems to happen to all these people. It seems to be the next logical step when you're so completely insulated from reality—by the money, by the people around you, by the whole thing, y'know,—how can you pull off the delicate balancing act of maintaining your contact with the everyday reality that keeps you a vital and a functioning artist, when you're living in that kind of a rarefied atmosphere?

Yeah.

And now, we're watching a lot of the punks go the same route. "Spoiled" is the unkind but operative word, I guess. When you get used to having a limousine anytime you want, it's pretty hard to stroll down to the candy store and talk to that kid like you described Bruce Springsteen doing.

There were always a certain number of rock people that Rod did relate to, and it seems he's pretty well cut off from them too. Apparently the English press pretty well hates him, as does, for the most part, the American press. In America he used to be a real press favorite, considered warm and downhome and all that. I would imagine he's wondering "Well, why are they writing this about me?" And I really don't think he knows.

I can remember in the summer of '72, when both the Stones and the Faces were on tour, Dave Marsh saying to me, "I'd take one Rod Stewart for five Mick Jaggers any day," and that was

how lots of people I knew, especially at Creem, *felt, because the Faces had that wonderful affability and by that time the Stones had just really started to become sort of … glaringly remote.*

Yeah, and that's where Rod's gotten to by now.

Whereas you could still imagine Rod Stewart, after the show, comin' over to the house and poppin' open a few beers and listenin' to some R&B records and havin' a good old time. But then, I also recall somebody saying the same thing to me about the Stones as opposed to the Beatles way back in 1964. And I got a real deja vu *sense that this was where the Clash were gonna end up when I went on tour with them in 1977. From what I know about the Rolling Stones and the Clash, and what I now know about Rod Stewart and the Faces, I think I* prefer *writing about Rod and the Faces. Ten years on the Clash (if they're still around) would make a helluva book. Right now they're sellouts, mostly, though they do seem to be human. The Faces always came off that way too, perhaps more than any other band I'd met to that time (or since, for that matter). They really were what they looked like: a bunch of clowns who wanted to have a wowzup and if they became bigshot international celebrities with fat bank accounts in the process, well, more's the hoopla. Ron Wood never seemed to give a damn except for his devotion to guitar playing, and all the Faces came off as distinctly* nice. *In rock 'n' roll you're never supposed to be a "nice guy", spells W-I-M-P for sure, but the only rock "stars" I ever met I liked or thought had any worth as people were all nice. I always found Rod a little remote, hard to talk with or get to somehow— even when I was doing stories for* Creem *and riding to gigs with them in an overcrowded limo where we drank and swapped stories, laughing about what cretinous creeps 90% of the other "stars" we met in this biz were.*

34

Yeah, well Rod still does that with his band on the road—he really does not play the star with them. But as for the show itself ... When Rod talks about the Faces now it's with the scorn of "Oh, that bunch of amateurs." Whereas his current show looks more like a TV spectacle, with all the costumes and stuff—that's his idea of what he *wants.*

I really thought he started moving toward that around the time of Atlantic Crossing, *when he was in the process of the final tour and split with the Faces in mid-'75. I thought the first step was that move: "Well, now I'm going to go to Muscle Shoals (Studio) and play with the big boys" —and what he and so many others failed to realize is that just because all these people made classic records ten years ago doesn't mean they're gonna do diddleyshit now.*

35

The people most against him now, he says, are members of society. But that doesn't worry him. He retains and cultivates the loyalty of the armed forces.

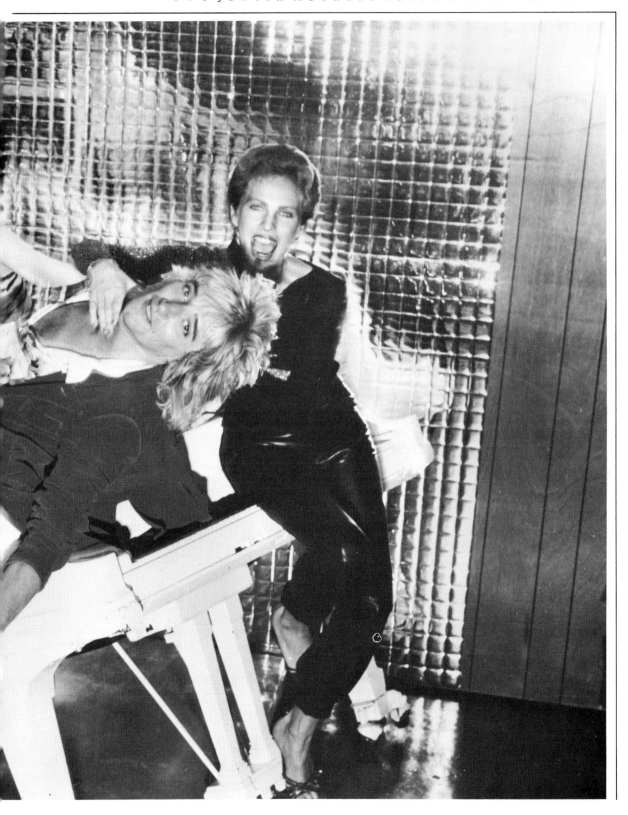

He still did some good songs in that period, but not as many, and when he lost that distinctive sound—

When he lost Ron Wood he lost his second mind.

He knows that. He will say that this band is superior musically, but what they don't have is the spark he and Ron Wood had together. He realizes that it isn't there.

I think initially he thought, "The Faces have gone as far as possible, and they're really sloppy, and slovenly." He said in interviews at the time, "Well, we'd go in and dick around the studio for a while and then spend the rest of the day down at the pub," and he wanted something that was really tight, and probably wanted to play with the "big boys," wanted to join the big leagues, and thought "Now I can make records like Otis Redding and all my heroes did, and Sam Cooke and that," and instead it seemed that ten gallons of linseed oil were poured into the mix and the guys at Muscle Shoals were just doin' a job, whereas the Faces had been slammin' it out, and that loosened Rod up.

I think he was probably getting a lot of pressure from Billy Gaff and Britt Ekland on the level of "Now's the time to become an international star, you don't need any of these flunkies who can't play very well, so make your move and we'll build you into a Hollywood glamour figure and then you'll be a solo act." And he did it, apparently quite willingly.

And don't forget the ego things that were going on all along from the Jeff Beck days that we, as fans on the outside, were never aware of, as well as a yearning, on their part, for a kind of legitimacy. The band thinks it will come their way if they do it according to a certain set of rules that, especially in the music industry, everybody believes in and just aren't true, or at least have nothing to do with rock 'n' roll.

Well, from his point of view and a business point of view, Rod probably did everything right. I bet Mick Jagger's well aware of all the conflicts in himself about it and that's what he's writing about, which sometimes makes for good music and other times doesn't. I don't get the sense that Rod's writing about conflicts, or is even aware that they exist.

That's why I said it's complex, because on one hand he wrote some of the most sensitive songs ever, yet on the other it keeps narrowing down to this roue image, on the cheapest possible level, as you said, like a hooker or something.

A very expensive hooker. That randy adventurer image was appealing, but the expensive hooker isn't.

It's dishonest too, because my theory about it is that 90% of these people are hookers, but a hooker who works the street is more honest about it. As a person grows older and older the more I'm sure it preys on them that they can't live up to an image they may have created, which eventually and manifestly becomes as apparent to everyone else as it is to them. Which all goes back to a self-destructive kind of narcissism that just closes in and in on itself, until all that's left is a shell.

It may be self-destructive as we view it, but not necessarily as Rod views it.

As a businessman or an artist?

I don't know if he thinks he's heading in that direction as an artist at all. He's hangin' out with who he wants to hang out with, he's sellin' more records than he's ever sold before, he's wonderin' why people like us are sitting around tryin' to figure out what's wrong with him.

38

But it's not just people like us—

Yeah, it is. More people buy his records today than they ever did. So they're obviously not seeing any of this; he's obviously pleasing millions of people.

But I'll bet you anything that if we ask different women what they think of him as a sex symbol, the great majority will say he's pathetic.

Could be, though I wouldn't necessarily bet on that; it depends on how wide a stratum you ask. People who aren't really rock 'n' rollers may not think so. And Rod probably thinks "Well, I made all this money so they're picking on me." See, I don't think he thinks there's been a great decline. Rod has got a lot, like Dylan has, of the rock 'n' roll businessman in him. If things change, he's gonna change right with 'em, to be on top of the charts. And I don't believe he thinks he necessarily has to lose artistically to do this; it's just, you know, keep in the swing of things.

If you go back to the songs on the period covered by Gasoline Alley, Every Picture Tells a Story *and* Never a Dull Moment, *and compare 'em to what he's doing now, well ...*

Except he'd probably say "You can't expect me to write the same kind of songs I was writing then because I'm ten years older," which is true in a way. Yet what he's substituted ... basically isn't worth much. But again I doubt he'd relate at all to the context in which we're discussing him. I don't think he'd even know what we're talking about. He's out there, and he's hobnobbing with all these famous names I'm sure he can charm the pants off of, and I'm sure he's thrilled to be in that company.

Well, that's the syndrome you see among media people in New York who end up being cheerleaders in the pages of Rolling Stone; *the poor kid gets in with the fast crowd and mistakes that for success, except he doesn't realize that almost all of them are poor kids who slid in on a wing and a prayer, so they're all conning each other, thinking the other one has something they don't. I read an article explaining that's what happened to Jack Nicholson and that's why his acting went to hell, but I bet you anything if it's true, and if Rod and Jack are friends, they don't necessarily perceive that in each other. Or maybe they really do and in fact they all know what a sham it is and are too embarrassed to say anything. But part of them, or him, is still that poor kid back there on* Gasoline Alley, *and he's afraid somebody's gonna come and shut him down because of that, so he has to keep up all these pretenses ... although this can get sticky; it becomes like psychoanalysis by proxy. I mean, you know the guy; I've only met him a few times peripherally during his career. But over the last few years—the music, lyrics, song titles—even the pictures of him on the album covers—he seems desperate. On* Blondes Have More Fun, *he seemed embarrassed and sheepish ...*

See, *I* don't think he thought he looked that way at all.

Really?

I think he thought he looked sexy as hell.

Jesus.

He's the guy that thinks these covers up, he's the guy that poses on the pink sheets in the valentine bed with the come-on look, and he's said in interviews that he gets off on that image. So I don't know how desperate you can be when you totally, willfully do that, and project yourself in that manner.

Maybe I'm just ridiculously naive, but when I see a picture like that, all I can see is a guy trying pathetically to shore up some image or some idea of his masculinity. I feel sorry for him!

39

Maybe deep down, but I don't think anybody twisted his arm to do it. I think he thought it was a hot idea.

In terms of marketing, for a lot of people it is. It's having Pat Benatar on the cover of Rolling Stone—*I thought it was so embarrassing, let alone offensive. As a man, the only thing I could feel it reaching in me was the part that hates women.*

Sure.

So ... maybe Rod's just another victim of the Sexual Revolution.

I don't even know how much we can get into that. All the times I've ever seen him he's been with women; he likes women. He may also like men, but I haven't seen it.

40

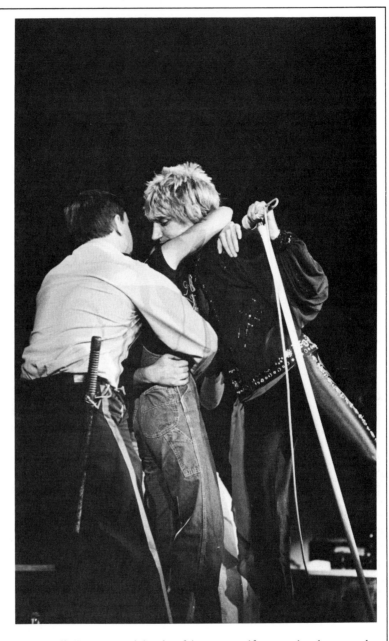

merely involve shaving off all the more subtle sides of the image itself ... Isn't that the process that happens with most of these people? For a while they maintain a balance that results in great songs or art, but later, with career pressures and because they do have an image, it narrows down until the image is changed; it's no longer this affable roue *who is also kind of a jerk sometimes like all of us once in a while, and gets hurt, y'know, and makes mistakes ... How marketable is that? How many people ultimately really wanna identify with that enough to buy it? Especially with the industry the way it's been getting the last few years. Folks wanna be with whoever wins. That fuckup/failure factor has gotta be absolute zero. And so it just gets worse and worse until you, meaning him or whoever's at the center in any given situation, are just that shell, and then you wake up one morning and say, "What happened?" Or you can't even say that. Maybe you think you are the image. That roue. And even if you are, is that worth being? For anything but money. Maybe what this all really means is that you and I would rather see him as that fuckup trying to write the letter in "You Wear It Well," or sittin' jackin' off to Playboy on a hot afternoon, whereas he would rather see himself, and most of his fans would rather see him, as The World's Greatest Lover, gadabout with Britt Ekland, or whatever it is he's supposed to be now. And you know where that leaves us, pal!*

Yeah! I think it was more a conscious decision by Rod and Britt and management to go the glamour route—to keep what he could of the old, but then go for glitter—

Because it was always there, the glitter and the glam and that—

But he really started flaunting it ...

Well, it's kind of taking the easy way out, y'know.

Then it became a merchandising method—

Sure. Everybody else used the same tactics. Look at what Lou Reed did on RCA.

I don't think Rod was consciously merchandising himself in the early days at all. And looking at it one way, it's been a spectacular success. Looking at it another way, it seems most of us who really cared at the beginning ... have to work real hard to care now. You might find a few songs here and there—

Maybe all it comes down to is that after a while you get tired.

I think in his mind he figures that he's reached the pinnacle of his career, is a millionaire several times over, and is well-liked in the community of Hollywood (which he has nothing but good things to say about). He probably thinks, ''I've done this, I'm above it now, I'm merely dabbling in it, I can't give it my full attention because I think I'm growing in other ways and this is a child's game and I'm an adult now, or I'm not connected like I used to be to it and I can't quite hack it so what do I do?''

In one sense that's probably the most likely and sensible assessment of the whole situation.

And now he's probably thinking, ''Well, maybe I should make a movie.''

If the poor boy just didn't look so unhappy! He brings out my Jewish Mother-instinct. Feed him some chicken soup! So, he wants a little caviar ...

We don't know that he's unhappy.

He sure looks it. Every time I see a photograph, every appearance ...

He may be unhappy that we're having discussions like *this*, not because of what he's doing!

Yeah, but if he's in the position you mentioned, then what the hell does he care? He's sittin' on top of all this money, he's one of the biggest stars in the world, why does he care what some punks with crappy equipment, idiot lyrics and no voice say about him—much less two rock critics? Or a billion punks and a million rock critics?

Oh, he does, though; they all do. He read some local review in a Florida paper, which was meaningless, and went off on a total rant about it. He reads everything.

Then obviously he still has an enormous stake of ego ...

Oh, yeah ...

44

But don't you see what you're saying—

Ego which is translated into anger.

—is almost two separate things, because if he is just dabbling and kicking back and enjoying his position as landed gentry, going to parties, and putting out a piece of product every once in a while for laughs, and then making some more money, he wouldn't be as upset as you say he is about all this.

That may be the situation, except I don't think necessarily that he regards it as a piece of product, not consciously. He must think it's pretty good stuff.

Well, it is, a lot of it's okay, I can listen to his 90 millionth Chuck Berry retread, a couple of times at least. If it came on a jukebox I wouldn't leave the room.

I'd much rather listen to that than Kenny Loggins, or Billy Joel, or Christopher Cross.

Sure. But you almost wouldn't, y'know, because there's something that comes out of songs like "D'Ya Think I'm Sexy" that's positively repellent if you hear it a certain way, which you sometimes certainly will. I don't go to singles bars … you know, it's the same kinda thing that makes you sorta queasy when a jeans commercial comes on TV.

Well, what I would say is that you almost wouldn't rather listen to him doing that because of the early stuff. He had a history of breaking your heart and he doesn't do that anymore, whereas Kenny Loggins never broke anybody's heart—there was never any to begin with, so there wasn't any loss. With most guys it wouldn't make much difference because they were never good to start with, but with Rod it does make a difference. There was something that we missed. And when it does show up on record and *is* still there, it makes you even more sad because it's not there all the way through. It's just there occasionally.

With so many of these people the impression you get is of an ongoing struggle. Dylan put out Self Portrait, *and everybody jumped down his throat, so he immediately put out* New Morning. *I don't think rock critics are important or have any power at all, and I think it's hilarious that these musicians have such gelatinous egos, but even with* Street-Legal *you could tell Dylan was trying to do something, struggling with himself in an attempt to communicate that's honest somewhere … Whereas Rod doesn't seem to be trying very hard on these albums at all …*

No. Not really. *Street-Legal* seemed to me like genuinely painful confusion: "I don't know what I'm doing but I'm trusting my instincts, that if I put all this shit down maybe it'll make some sort of sense, but anyway I'm in anguish"—I don't get that sort of feeling from Rod at all. These albums aren't the anguished portrait of a person who's really consciously mixed-up. More that he's entering that vast MOR rock area—

Madame Tussaud's.

—where the big bucks are, and he probably sees not a hell of a lot wrong with it, thinks it's a logical progression and why should we be upset?

Well, maybe I'm simple-minded, or an absolutist or a fanatic or something, but it's always hard for me to imagine someone simultaneously having that attitude and yet still being concerned about themselves and their future as an artist. Certain things you've said tonight make it seem like he is.

Well, he *is*, but I think everybody has that sort of … I mean Dylan, throughout the

Sixties, was continually saying "Don't listen to leaders" and then when it looked like he wasn't gonna be a leader he panicked totally, y'know, and wanted *desperately* to be a leader. I don't think that's so unusual ...

Well, that was a bit of a different case, though. Do you really think, from the beginning, that Rod was as calculating as Dylan was?

No. But I think once you're on top, you wanna stay there. No matter what you think, no matter what you've said in the past, if you start slipping, you wanna be Number One. That's certainly the case with Dylan. If Christianity doesn't keep him on top of the charts, the next album won't be Christianity, I bet you anything.

Yeah, but there are other things these people could do. I mean, if he really just wanted to be on top of the charts, he could make a Bee Gees album.

Somehow I think that people saying "Don't follow leaders" when they are the leaders, is like rich people saying that money doesn't matter. Sure, it doesn't matter if you've got it! And they probably believe it when they say it, but ... to the guy who isn't the Number One, who doesn't have the money—

Well, it's just like the Clash, saying all these same sorts of things as Dylan did in the Sixties about individualism and freedom, no leaders blah blah, but then they take this sort of Elder States-men position in a lot of their songs, to the point you can almost hear 'em lecturing younger bands in the lyrics.

Which is a tension that can work in art, but I don't think there is that kinda tension in Rod's art. Not very much. I wish there were.

In fact the tension that is there, that I pick up from it, is just so—icky, is the only word I can think of, I mean, a song like "D'Ya Think I'm Sexy," and don't get me wrong, I like it, I like that arrangement and—

It's catchy, yeah.

But when I really let myself listen to those words and think about what they mean, it's just "Yecchhh!" And after thinking about what's in there that does appeal to so many people and why, is when you wanna make plans to leave the human race.

Well, it's just a complete ripoff of the Stones' disco hit.

Yeah, but theirs was undoubtedly a ripoff of somebody else too, who was probably black to boot. The Stones are the original ripoff artists, so who cares?

Yeah, but I'll betcha that's why he made a disco song—because the Stones got a Number One single. It's a good one, on a certain level it's real catchy—

But look who it's aimed at.

Yet he is still capable, maybe it's just reflex action or whatever, but "Oh God, I Wish I Was Home Again" really moves me, it's a good song, and although it's for-mulaic he makes it *work*. Whereas the other songs on the album are just like a lead quarter, they just don't have anything to 'em at all. He doesn't even sound like he can bear to sing them, or make them sincere, he doesn't even seem to want to bother.

Yeah, but what was that song on the Blondes *album, "Sleazy Weekend," if people think that's great songwriting, then what if he sank to the level of turning out whole albums of songs like that one, with the sleaze factor quantified, sort of the LP equivalent of Guccione's* Caligula?

46

That's enough to give you nightmares! What a horrifying notion.

Yeah! You'd *be appalled! But I betcha* they *wouldn't! Ha! Who's the jaded sicko then, in your scheme of things?*

I don't even want to think about it.

Right. And for sure you'd throw in the towel on him forever. But people who idolize Rod for everything that currently nauseates us might even push him up into the even more mega-platinum brackets! Because he has this image, this thing he's supposed to be, and finally it doesn't matter that once it might actually have been at least somewhat real, the fact is that's what the fan is buying in the first place: a picture of how life supposedly is, or should be, or wishes it could be for him. It's as if everybody were steadily growing half-deaf, then a little more each day, so the drums and trumpets and TV commercials have gotta keep being retuned, amped higher until they're at a level that quite recently would have been considered past the pain threshold. That's what images are all about, and talent or inspiration or passion has nothing to do with it. Directly the opposite. It's freezing the self for vending purposes. Now, I ask you: who, after they've been sifted and recycled through every deli, dental waiting room, in-flight headset and contempo-muzak phonehold in the world, is actually gonna be sitting there in a few years, still listening to these recent Rod Stewart albums and gleaning some soul sustenance therefrom? Can you find or show me somebody, anybody, anywhere in the world? 'Cause if you can then we should probably be interviewing her or him instead of each other.

Well, no, I can't, except for, well, actually ...

C'mon, give ...

Well, actually, yeah, it might be a little embarrassing or a complete waste of time, but ... *me!*

49

Unca Scrooge

Never Had a Kidhood Like This

CHAPTER III

I n a way it's not surprising that Rod Stewart should have turned out to be the most absolutely conventional kind of rock star during his post-Faces career (though for me it began either with Atlantic Crossing, which contained all the elements of the eventual transformation, or its predecessor Smiler, which was the first piece of pure product he released in his life—though hardly the last). But nobody turns into the person he ultimately becomes (and really was all along) overnight. I don't hate Rod Stewart, but as Paul says it's damn hard to like him much. He is certainly the quintessence of the corporate rock superstar: he even still has a personality! Gets all bent outa shape over things: reviews, punks, this, that, but even though I personally believe he has nigh totally and irretrievably betrayed his considerable gifts, he is still more human to me than Mick Jagger, and I still like and listen to the Stones' albums where I never bother now with Rod's. He may have become more of a businessman than a musician at this point, but somehow he still comes across with the personal touch in interviews, and there's damn few that do. They're post-human. They have finally in every respect of their real lives become what you see on The Midnight Special each Friday night.

Rod can, I think, continue for a long time as well. He doesn't have drug problems, and even his drinking is not that big a deal. This man is going to live to a ripe old age, father several children, and you can be damn sure of sons; if he has to produce twelve girls first, he'll have that little Rodders there beside him.

51

The reason I can say this of a man I never really even interviewed and last spoke to six years ago for two minutes is that I have interviewed every rock star who ever lived and like anything else they eventually begin to break down into types.

Rod, as a type, has about as much to do with the sensibility defined as rock 'n' roll as, oh, I dunno, it's hard to even think of anybody to tell the truth, because it's a spirit that seeps in or you always had a little bit in there. And this spirit—if it is one thing—is not conservative. Rod is conservative to the bone. From the cradle to the grave. Except for one short period in his life, corresponding to his membership in/leadership of a group called the Faces, who were about as conservative as a careening firetruck with one rear axle loose and the driver floorboarding it anyway. As much as any band I have ever seen in my life, the Faces embodied the spirit of rock 'n' roll. Not real long on your highflown poetic/collegiate or conceptual/artschool ideas and complete slobs on a "musicianship" level, which is a consideration that never had anything to do with rock 'n' roll from day one, they were the core of the sound and a certain who-gives-a-damn attitude that was so cocky it didn't even bother to try for Menacing (like everybody else did) or Privileged (always one of the most loathsome things about the Scene and worse now than ever). That band took more abuse than absolutely any other band of their stature during the Seventies. The reason the Faces were treated like shit by everybody from Rod himself to their very own press releases, was that they were real in an era when almost nobody surviving was. They were subversive, without turning it into some stupid "crusade." They were an insult to everything rock represented in the Seventies, a pie square in the kisser. They paid for that. It was noticed. Everything is in the music business, where the curators may let you run hogwild or appear to, or kill yourself (which they absolutely love because man does it move that product). The Faces were not a product, nor could they have become "corporate." It was just not in them, and especially since they never made any big deal about it, they had as much integrity as any band I've ever seen. They had far more of it all the way down the line than, say, the Clash. Practically everyone in New Wave is a complete hypocrite; they are just like everybody else in the music business, which itself as a corporate entity would market the Guyana tapes with disco backbeat overdubbed if they thought they could make a dime out of it. The musicians themselves would put on batwings, get any kind a haircut, sing nothing but Nazi marching songs or lounge band ooze, let Percy Faith produce all their albums with Ray Conniff sitting in, any humiliation or brutalism or nightmare you can think of, if they thought it gave them one chance in ten of getting to be the next Cheap Trick. They are all compleat chameleons in a business which is one of the few corporate entities on earth where absolutely anyone can and will be called an artist. You know, like Jimmy Osmond. He's an artist. Just like Miles Davis. And if Rod often looks like the spittin' physical embodiment of a Colonial plantation master, you must credit him with a weird sort of integrity. Certainly not on his records, which are pandering junk, or his stage show, in which he endeavors to be Al Jolson in Las Vegas with a little of Jayne Mansfield thrown in: enough to make you cringe in embarrassment for him. It's in his stance, himself; from First Step and the first solo album to this day, Rod has stood up to the industry and called his own shots and got what he wanted without ever really posing, because those awful poses you see onstage and album covers are the person. What he has become is what he always wanted to be and made no bones about that either. All appearances to the contrary, Rod Stewart is not a prostitute. He thinks Hollywood is just dandy and hell he doesn't even wanna be in movies. He only really wants four or five things from life. One is all that glamour including conspicuous consumption of pussy boys hor ha har nudge wink. Two is to stay a multimillionaire for the rest of his life. Three is to be able to make music which means put out records and sing before large audiences for the rest of his life, even though he has 90% lost the ability to feel a note of it and I doubt it'll come back ever and I don't think he knows or cares just as long as those notes, beats, cues, choreographed chorus lines and other technical minutae are in the exact place which he has concluded is right according to the Book Of Rules, which also says that they must come out exactly alike, in the same order and

52

measure and consistency each time. Four is Scotland and, in close association, the game of football.
Five and every bit as important is to put down those deep family roots complete with a smoothly
functioning domestic outlay including those sons, dogs, aunts and uncles and the like. Don't dare
leave out the hearth because he knows a home, unlike band or car, ain't no precision machine but a
beating heart. I suspect that the less he cares about any vestiges of heart in the music the more this
cozy berth will be the joy of his life. The reason Rod wants to live that way in an age when the
nuclear family would seem to be an endangered species is that he wants to end up exactly like his
father, except one hell of a lot richer.

RODERICK DAVID STEWART WAS BORN DURING THE LAST MONTH OF WORLD WAR II, on January 10, 1945, one-half hour after a German V2 rocket fell on the local police station in Highgate, North London. Later he would say, sincerely: "I've always thought that I was very lucky because that bomb fell just a stone's throw from where I lived. I've sort of had that feeling that I nearly didn't make it."

One supposes it also is the kind of primal event which would predispose someone to later play most things very close to the vest. If Rod has a religion I would say it is probably his father, Robert Stewart, who worked as a builder in Scotland, later bringing his wife Elsie and their four children—Don, Bob, Mary, and Peggy—to live in London. Somewhere between the passionate fealties he feels for his father and football lies the nation of Scotland, where Rod has ways regretted he was not born. He has always been a fanatical supporter of all things Scottish: the football teams, the wearing of the plaid and even the National Seal (as soon as he was rich enough for his first mansion he bought the biggest one he could find and hung it prominently in his living room). He refers to himself as Scottish and of course owns a home there.

One gathers that his family made up for the insult of Rod being the sole member born on London soil by giving him just about anything he ever wanted. By all accounts including his own, "I was a spoiled brat." He enjoyed the remotest possible forming ground from your standard English working-class hardscrub gehenna from which they're all supposed to break like convicts into rock stardom.

Rod has always been Middle Class and proud. His family lived above a little store they owned in the Archway Road in North London, where they sold newspapers, magazines, tobacco and candy. They had to rise before dawn to organize that day's supply of morning papers and weekly magazines, and years later when the area was redeveloped and the shop itself demolished Mr. and Mrs. Stewart bought themselves a house in North London. Our Sex Symbol seems to have grown up in an atmosphere devoid of trauma or the kind of ugly incidents John Lennon later sang of and Sid Vicious never got a chance to. Although one of his British biographers calls him "one of the most evasive people I have ever interviewed about his childhood," Rod has admitted that his early life was content, ordinary, and conventional. As he said years later, "The only thing I worry about is me dad. If I upset me dad, then I'm really in trouble. He's nearer to me than anything." Twice in his career he's blundered into shaming his father. In December 1973 national papers reported that Rod had supposedly taken "porno photos" (hell, they were on a big foldout wall poster that came inside every copy of the Faces' *A Nod is as Good as a Wink*, and consisted of the standard Instamatic snapshots bands have always been damn near *expected* to take of themselves doing Rude Things with nubile groupies in hotel rooms). Rod told *Disc and Music Echo* that "I went into hiding for five days after that. My dad rang up and said, 'Where's me son?' I didn't dare see him. He still hits me, and I'm 28 years old." Later around the time of *Foot Loose and Fancy Free* the dailies leaked an "illegitimate

53

Rod and Steam Package
Contzeres; *left to right Long
John Baoedry, Jully Driscoll and
Brian Auguer.*

child" story and while he boasted to *Creem* magazine that if the fans had only listened a little more attentively to "Jo's Lament" theyd've learned it from *Gasoline Alley* in 1970, he admitted elsewhere that "Since that was in the papers, I haven't spoken to him in three weeks. I daren't phone up."

Their happiest times were generally at Christmas when the whole family would gather round and sing old Al Jolson songs, which was probably his first exposure to music. Although they weren't a family of "music lovers" they did have a complete set of Jolson's albums and later Rod said that "My mum and dad, my whole family were Al Jolson freaks. My brother John does a very good impersonation, and so did my grandfather at one time. That was well before I had any idea I was going to come into this business myself. I got so bowled over by him. The more I read about him, I sort of flatter myself and try to compare myself to him. I've got one thing in common with him. That's that I can't bear seeing empty seats at a gig we're playing. I have terrible dreams about that. Jolson used to have that one. It's incredible when you think that he had no mike and could reach an audience of 2,000. I don't sing any Al Jolson numbers and I don't even try to sing any. It was his attitude to his audience that probably influenced me more. It was the way he sold a number that I thought was magnificent." And there is no reason not to suspect that on all those post-Faces tours where Rod worked his audiences in the way Paul describes in the first chapter, it just might be Stewart's Conceit that he was the legitimate heir to Jolson's showbiz mantle.

His parents were stunned, though, when Rod finally did tell them that he wanted a career in music, because "We were a football family. All of us were football crazy," and they took it for granted that someday Rod was gonna lite up the Stewart name by becoming the family's first professional football star. He's been going to football games with Pops his entire life, when he visits home now the two always go to Arsenal's home games, and Rod often plays for Highgate Redwing in the Finchley and District League on Saturday mornings. He'd been good enough when he was in school to be offered a trial in the schoolboys' international side, but that dry run of the Dream got doused in short order when the Winklepicker Shoes the li'l hepster was wearing everywhere gave him ingrown toenails. During a teenage, post-school period of aimlessness, however, Dad saw his chance and when Rod was weak and vulnerable enough, he was trundled down and placed in front of papers which he then signed, with Brentford, who were in the 2nd Division. Some papers have reported Rod as even playing a few games in their "A" team and Reserves, but Rod said "It was my Dad's idea. I signed on as a professional and they paid me eight pounds for a seven-day week. I cleaned the first team's boots and cleaned out the lockers and that's about all. I gave it up after three weeks—never having kicked a ball" so tuff porkduke ya ole bastid. He kept his yap shut 'round diddley Daddy bout it, but since he "just didn't feel like getting up at eight o'clock every morning and doing all those things" (as only a moron would), he began to think, "A musician's life is a lot easier than all these things, and I can also get drunk." He still says "They're the only two things I can do actually: play football and sing."

Since he's graduated to landed gentry, he's gotten into the habit of doing things like flying from New York to Scotland, sitting in a hotel room to watch one game, then flying straight back; or rigging telephone hookups whereby he can lounge at home in L.A. where the Rams jam and catch all the action in games in divers distant climes.

LESTER BANGS

54

55

Wake Up, Rodney,

I Think It's Time For You To Record

CHAPTER IV

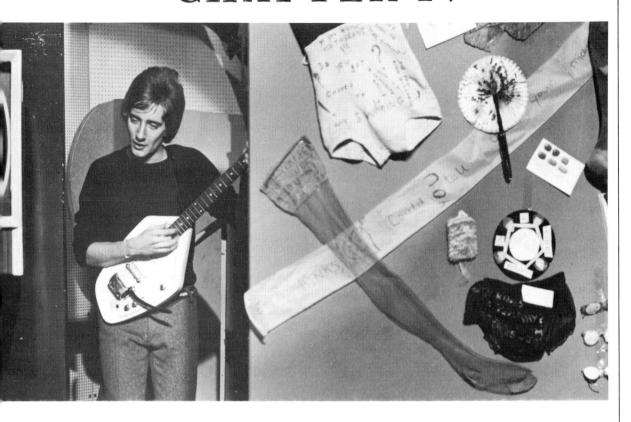

O NCE HE GOT CLEAR OF FAMILY AND FOOTBALL (AT LEAST TEMPORARILY), THE NEXT
step for Rod was a natural one in the early Sixties: folkie quasi-beatnikdom. He was a
big fan of Ramblin' Jack Elliot and an obscure figure named Wizz Jones, apparently a
real busker. Rod has bragged about years of bumming around Europe with Jones, who
has since thanked Rod for all the free plugs but told interviewers he can't remember
ever meeting him in the early days. Rod did once participate in the famous Alder-
maston Ban-the-Bomb marches, though (he brags) more as a way of getting laid than
out of any political convictions (which is something he's never held, having in his
time supported everybody from George McGovern to British racist Enoch Powell,
however briefly in all cases). That apparently was where he first sang in public, and
since he was apparently learning *guitar*, maybe he did blang and yelp some sweet
proto-flowerchild into doin the thang while Bertrand Russell looked on approvingly.

It's hard to say much you'd stand by regarding this period, because since Rod's
such a tetchy cuss he saw to it that all his early bios were fulla lies making him sound
like some banty Kerouac. Dylan did the same thing, they all do it, but it's horse ma-

nure. Even if he did (as he also advertised) get 86'd outa Spain for being some leftoid undesirable, there were clean sheets 'n' a smiling Mum to tuck 'im in right back there on the Archway Road, which was where he lived all through his early career in the music business.

Even though the first record he bought was an Eddie Cochran single, he turned for inspiration to the likes of Elliot and Jones. Rod came up in the early Sixties, folk era anyway, and he was always more of a folkie than a rocker, just a little too late for the Teds and too young to hone his chops during the Beat(les) Boom. "Folk songs, that's what they are, just folk songs I like," he would later tell *Rolling Stone* of his first solo album in 1970. His first instrument was the five-string banjo, which he'd later play on one track of *First Step*, but he first worked as a harmonica player, in a group called Jimmy Powell and his Dimensions. "He was the first in a long line of British Ray Charles imitators, also the worst," Rod laughed to *Rolling Stone*. "He wouldn't let me sing; I had a horrible voice then."

It took him a while to get it together on harmonica too. Once the Dimensions opened a club in Colyer for the Stones and Rod watched their set, picking up tips from Jagger's performance: "An important thing I learned at that time was how to play harmonica properly. That was through watching Mick Jagger do it. I realized I had been sucking when I should have been blowing and vice versa."

Rod himself got noticed at that Colyer club date by Long John Baldry, who was singing at the time with the Rhythm 'n' Blues All Stars, led by Cyril Davies.

Davies died in January 1964, and Baldry turned the All Stars into Long John Baldry's Hoochie Coochie Men. Legend has it Baldry and Rod first met on the platform of the Twickenham railway station after a night at Eel Pie Island, a popular R&B club. "Young man," Baldry supposedly said, "it sounds like you've got a good voice there for singing R&B."

It sure beat working for his brother or painting signs in London, which was how he'd been earning money while still living at home, so Rod gave that up at the age of nineteen, and became a professional musician on a regular wage of £35 a week. He became alternating vocalist, doing the fast numbers while Baldry (the purist) saved the the slow blues for himself, and often got individual billing ("Rod the Mod," "The Mod's Delight"). According to one account: "He was dressed as Rod the Mod with a muffler around his neck, trousers that hung suspended over his shoes, and hair like a sheaf of corn that'd been run over by a tractor. And he had this strange habit of hiding his face when he sang, looking down at his feet or under his armpit—but never *at* the audience. It looked very cultivated; the truth was he was still very shy and nervous."

He later told *N.M.E.* about his first performance: "The first song I ever sang professionally on the stage ... was 'Night Time is the Right Time.' And I took a leaper to do it. I remember Cliff Barton gave me a leaper because I was so scared. I was up for about three days but I didn't half sing that number ... Then I started doing 'Tiger in Your Tank,' which was my show-stopper.

Rod had first heard the blues on a Big Bill Broonzy record when he was twelve years old, but now he was learning quickly from Baldry, although "I never really considered myself a blues singer. I still don't—I'm a folk singer if I'm anything," he told *Melody Maker* years later when with the Faces. But "I was trying so hard to sound black it was embarrassing—when I sang things like 'Midnight Hour.' On the other hand, Cyril Davies played some better blues than anything that ever came out of Chicago."

He stayed with Baldry a year. The Hoochie Coochie Men broke up when Baldry

58

went to appear in a Jack Good TV special *Around the Beatles*, which was shown around the world but did absolutely nothing for Rod's mentor's career. "John was always very easily led," Rod has commented. Perhaps the best summation of Baldry's talents came from Greil Marcus in his *Creem* review of a Baldry LP (one side produced by Rod) in 1971: *It Ain't Easy,* the new here-he-is-folks LP by (sort of) fabled Long John Baldry ... is the first chance in many a year us benighted Americans have had to delight in the dues-paying authenticity of this English legend.... The hang-over from his Englebert Humperdinck period (just recently abandoned as plastic, man, not where I'm really at, my heart belongs to the blues, you dig) is all too obvious.... The story on the back of the LP speaks with wonder about this man who could kick around for a decade or more, working out with Mick Jagger, Rod Stewart, Elton John, Julie Driscoll, many others, but never make it himself. He may be a great guy, but I think the reason he never made it is that he hasn't got it."

Rod did and through his tenure with Baldry he tried to pursue a simultaneous solo career, making an appearance on the BBC's *Beat Room* show on August 6, 1964, going down to Portsmouth to be on Southern TV, up to Newcastle for a guest appearance on a children's TV program, and recording his first single (although he had made an uncredited appearance in an earlier-released duet with Baldry), "Good Morning Little Schoolgirl," on Sept. 10, 1964. The circumstances of this session are so extraordinary that they are hereby quoted in full from George Tremlett's British biography *The Rod Stewart Story*:

> Rowlands and Wright [Rod's managers at the time] had produced the whole session for 36.50 pounds using top session men, all of whom were paid the current Musicians Union rate for the job. Bobby Graham was on drums; Brian Daly on guitar; Rod Guest on piano—on bass was none other than John Paul Jones, who is now with Led Zeppelin. 'I see from this that we paid the musicians a total of 35 pounds and that another 1.50 pounds was spent on drinks,' said Rowlands....
>
> But those details did not even hint at the real problems that he and Wright had that September day down at Decca's Number Two Studio; a day when all the difficulties of having to manage a sometimes temperamental artiste like Rod Stewart became most apparent....
>
> The studio had been booked from 11 A.M. Wright and Rowlands turned up on time. So did the producer. And so did all the session musicians—but there was no Rod Stewart to be seen. "We had found a number of new songs for Rod to record and he was supposed to have learnt them," said Wright. "And we'd all arranged to meet down at the studio, having had all the orchestrations done for the songs ... usually studio sessions are very orderly and disciplined, and it was unknown for anyone to be late for a session. To be even five minutes late for a session was a sin in those days. Anyway, after we'd all been waiting about an hour I thought we had better phone his home. And I went to the phone. I called his parents' shop ..."
>
> It was Mrs. Stewart who answered the phone and Wright asked: "Is Rod there?"
>
> "He's fast asleep in bed," she said.
>
> Controlling his temper, Wright said: "But he's supposed to be making his record. All the musicians are waiting in the studio ... we're all down here waiting for him."

59

"Well, I'd better go and get him out of bed," said Mrs. Stewart, and about three minutes later a husky voice came to the phone and Rod said: "Oh Christ, yes—I'm sorry. I forgot. I got home very late from Eel Pie Island. I didn't get in until four o'clock and I've overslept."

"Jump in a taxi and get down here as fast as you can," said Wright, explaining that they would all wait for him.

"I can't afford a taxi," said Stewart.

"Well, I'll pay. You get the taxi, and I'll pay him when you get here," said Wright, beginning to be aware that in spite of the high wages he earned with Baldry, Rod was ultra-careful with his money. About an hour after that Rod arrived—by which time Rowlands and Wright had decided that shouting and screaming would do no good to any of them.

"We didn't want to upset him—late though we were. We wanted to get a good session done," said Wright. "Everyone was relatively calm after Rod arrived and repeated his apologies—until we asked him about the songs that we had orchestrated..."

There was a silence.

"Those songs you gave me—I haven't learned them," said Stewart. "I decided that I didn't like them ..."

"What's wrong with them?" asked Rowlands and Wright almost simultaneously, the atmosphere in the studio getting decidedly more heated.

"They're too commercial," said Rod.

"By this time we were very close to screaming the studios down," said Wright, who nevertheless asked Rod if he would like to tell them what songs he *would* like to record.

"I've heard a couple of good songs on a new LP by Sonny Boy Williamson," said Stewart.

"Well, where's the music?" asked Wright.

Another silence, though briefer this time—as Rod went on to say that he had seen a copy of the album in the window of a local record shop on his way down to the studio.

"I will go down and buy the album, then we can hear it—then they can busk it," said Stewart.

"By this time, I was completely speechless," said Wright.

But Rod was not. "Can you lend me the two pounds to go and buy it?" he said. Which they did. He returned about five minutes later with the album, which was then played through the speakers into the studio by the Decca technicians—and about five minutes after they had heard the track the hired session men started "busking." About another five minutes later after just one take—though with words that were not quite perfect—Rod finished the first track. And that was how "Good Morning Little Schoolgirl" came to be recorded.... The B-side was recorded that same day, and that was another track from the same Sonny Boy Williamson LP—"I Am Gonna Move To The Outskirts Of Town"....

Unfortunately for Rod, the Yardbirds released *their* version of the exact same song as a single that same month, and unfortunately for both, they both flopped. Though the press release accompanying Rod's version remains an interesting document. In it,

60

Rod was quoted as saying: "A white person can sing the blues with just as much conviction as a Negro. All these coloured singers singing about 'walking down the railroad'... they've never walked down a railroad track in their lives. Nor have I. You've got more to sing the blues about in the Archway Road, near my home, than on any railroad track I know!"

Rod also played a few gigs in late '64 and early '65 before joining Steampacket, a group put together by Giorgio Gomelsky, a legendary impresario and record producer. He managed the Crawdaddy club where the Stones and Yardbirds played in the early days—a scene Rod was never really part of—and produced the *Five Live Yardbirds* album, which of course was a turning point in the history of rock 'n' roll, featuring the Yardbirds' first version of "Schoolgirl" and some of Eric Clapton's earliest-recorded and most widely imitated guitar work.

Gomelsky was the kind of real Euro-beatnik Rod had pretended to be, and also managed the Brian Auger Trinity, later recruiting Julie Driscoll from presidential post in the Yardbirds fan club to sing on two albums and their hit version of Dylan's "This Wheel's on Fire." Steampacket was conceived as a kind of Super (White) Band version of something like the Ike and Tina Turner Review, with vocals by Driscoll, and Long John Baldry, back from failure. Baldry insisted Gomelsky hire Stewart as well, and Rod ended up doing most of the male vocals. Auger: "It was like a package thing. There was me playing more or less jazz stuff; there was Julie doing rhythm and blues things from Wilson Pickett through Aretha Franklin to Nina Simone and Oscar Brown ... who was singing Tamla things and straight Chicago Blues."

They did a brief tour which ended at the London Palladium, where they supported the Stones and the Walker Brothers. Once again Rod picked up inspiration from Mick Jagger, since as John Pidgeon has written: "Watching the crowd react to the Stones gave Rod his first taste of crowd hysteria."

Then, however, the Yardbirds broke in America, and Gomelsky followed them over, causing Steampacket to founder. Rod did record with them, some abysmal tapes made by Gomelsky and released in 1971 as part of a series of albums called *Rock Generation* on the French BYG label. Rod also cut two solo singles, "The Day Will Come" b/w "Why Does It Go On" with orchestral backing, and "Shake" b/w "I Just Got Some" with the Brian Auger Trinity, both for EMI's Columbia label. The first Rod considered a "concession to pop," since at the time he thought of himself (and was widely considered) as a "purist." The second single, however, was an important one for him, in that it represented his discovery of Sam Cooke, his greatest influence as a vocalist (where Jolson influenced him as a showman). He called it a "crossing of the water."

By March '66 Rod was out of Steampacket, either fired (according to him) or having quit (according to Auger), and later summed up his feelings about the entire experience as "a typical example of a band getting up on-stage and playing other people's hits—it wasn't the most original band to be in." Then he made one flop single with a similar band, Shotgun Express, "I Could Feel the Whole World Turn Around." They played a few gigs and broke up: guitarist Peter Green and Mick Fleetwood forming Fleetwood Mac; bassist Dave Ambrose joining Brian Auger's Trinity; and Rod Stewart joining the Jeff Beck Group, where he hooked up with an old guitarist/bassist friend (whose own Birds had recently fallen apart) named Rod Wood.

LESTER BANGS

61

Bowling For Supergroups:
The Beck Years

CHAPTER V

THERE WAS REALLY VERY LITTLE REASON TO SUSPECT, ON THE BASIS OF EITHER OF THE two Jeff Beck Group LPs on Epic with Rod singing and Wood on bass, that Stewart would ever achieve what he later did as a vocalist, much less songwriter. Everybody in the band was at loose ends in a way, and the Jeff Beck Group was just trying to get "Super" added in there, like Beck, Bogart and Appice later. Personally, I've always preferred "Love Is Blue" to any of the Group's nonsense, not to mention *Blow By Blow*. The only good thing Beck did after leaving the Yardbirds was quit playing entirely for awhile, as he confided to an interviewer from *Zig Zag* magazine in August 1969: "I didn't even touch my guitar, and when I came to play again I was hopeless, but I started to do session work with Jimmy Page."

"Beck's such a good guitar player," Stewart told Mac Garry for *Creem* in an unusually candid interview late in 1971, "wish he'd give himself a kick up the arse."

Many people would of course say the same thing about Rod right now—I can just imagine what Ron Wood, not to mention the other ex-Faces, must be thinking when they hear Rod's pieces of product closer to peroxide than music—but none of these boys were at all sure they'd end among the gentry back in '68; hell, they hustled their tonsils and guitar cases around so much from group to group and country to country that nobody, least of all themselves, could've even called 'em *landed*.

Fret-King Beck himself got 86'd from the Yardbirds in the final months of 1966, right after being voted England's most popular guitarist in one rockmag poll. He got nervous as you would, saying at the time that gee he sure wouldn't mind if Ray Charles, Ike and Tina Turner or Phil Spector gave him a buzz with offers of some (any?) kinda employment, though maybe on the other hand his real future lay in the movies, whether as soundtrack-scorer, actor or director he never made clear.

Along came producer Mickie Most, a legendary schlockmeister who all agreed knew his way around a pop hit and back again, and Beck rushed out "Hi Ho Silver Lining," a slice of anti-groupie misogyny b/w the immortal "Beck's Bolero," a Jimmy Page can-do which my old friends back home treated like it tromped Django Reinhardt and Charlie Christian combined to one puddle of candyass. Beck basically knew the A-side was worthless (the B-side was an exercise to keep the fingers from getting arthritic). "I was a star again; I didn't dislike the tune, and I tried, but playing my style across a song like that just doesn't make it," he said later—but it worked: Number Eight on the British charts and several weeks' run on *Top of the Pops* (Limey *American Bandstand*, sorta).

Still, you gotta show the consumers a band to really convince them you care about anything but their shekels. Early in 1967 Beck began performing live almost as soon as he started auditioning prospects. Initial lineup: J.B. and Ron Wood on guitars; Rod Stewart singing; one Jet Harris on bass; and Viv Prince, whose own finest hour was ranking as one of the ugliest mugs on the cover of the first Pretty Things album back in '65, on drums. There were problems all the way, but things were particularly shaky at first, especially with drummers. They went through no less than six different drummers, including Mickey Waller and Aynsley Dunbar, and were just about to hire Scott Asheton in desperation and because he knew the Louie Bellson solo from "Skin Deep" triplet-to-paradiddle, when one Roger Cooke (later of Blue Mink) saved the day by walking into the room and announcing: "I'm British, Asheton's American. You work it out in terms of U.S. record sales." He was hired and stayed.

Not surprisingly, none of this was stardust-encouraging to Rod, who later told Garry that he stayed with Beck back then more out of pity than anything else: "We thought we'd better help him out ... I mean, for a guitar player like that to come out with a thing like 'Hi Ho Silver Lining'—it was a crime."

Beck either didn't know this or didn't care, and one can just imagine Mickie Most's then-current opinion of one Rod Stewart's commercial possibilities. Rod himself just looked at the current state of his recording career—which hadn't amounted to much—as journeyman's work, marking time. They cut Graham (Yardbirds' "For Your Love" and 1981 Ramones producer) Gouldman's "Tallyman," more fluff off a demo. Beck, according to Rod, "didn't say anything, but just left it up to Mickie's judgment. I made the record and sort of closed my eyes." No wonder—with lyrics on the order of "shoes and socks, pretty frocks in the latest styles." Rod: "That was the worst of the three singles."

Cooke apparently couldn't take it anymore, so he quit. Re-enter Mickey Waller. It made little difference who was doing what on the A-sides of these things, beyond "Jeff Beck" on the label and maybe a hotshit guitar solo tossed off (*cf.* "Tallyman"), for absolutely no reason beyond whim, one afternoon's chemical happenstance, or natural perversity. Speaking of which, next up was the dreaded/legendary "Love Is Blue." Now, I have always wanted to think that Jeff Beck conceived the idea of cutting "Love Is Blue" all by himself and did the whole thing on purpose just to fuck up Yardbirds fans and tell the whole world that he was the greatest guitarist alive and who cares because he was so cool he could actually get away with something like this. (I guess I'll always remain just a hopeless romantic.)

On the other hand, maybe you wouldn't mind cutting your "Love Is Blue" if it bought you the time and latitude to do what you really wanted to do. If so, you'd be following in the grand tradition of Beck-Stewart *et. al. ca.* 1967–8, when they put whatever they damn well pleased on the B-sides of those singles because M. Most had done his day's work and couldn't give a damn. Flip over "Tallyman" and you got to hear "Rock My Plimsoul," in which Beck, Stewart, Wood and Dunbar'd begun to sound like a real band, and which Rod was still proud of years later. I don't like it, but what do I know? I never liked *Truth.*

Jeff did eventually admit that in even his estimation that album was, as Mac Garry put it, "sort of thrown together and included a couple of filler tracks just to make it a reasonable length." What, they actually didn't think J.B. & Co.'s version of "Old Man River" would stand the test of time right alongside the Stooges' "L.A. Blues?" Garry liked *Truth* better than its author ("magnificent," he gushed three years later), and Rod liked it better than Jeff as well, though according to Mac "he agreed that they just went into the studio and bashed down a load of tracks that they'd been playing for almost a year." Rod: "But I really dug it at the time, even 'Greensleeves.' "

Maybe he was right. I had a phone interview with John Coltrane for *Jazz & Pop* magazine two months after it was released, and when I mentioned his version of "Greensleeves" on 1962's *Africa/Brass,* all he'd say was, "They cut me. White boys too. I think I better get off and go hit the woodshed."

One thing was for sure: America liked *Truth.* As a matter of fact, it was, along with the works of Cream and the first Led Zeppelin album, among the first artifacts we were lucky enough to hear representative of that burgeoning miracle, The (Usually) British Superband. Everybody bought it. Garry said they "set the country on fire." (Trane: "Damn, beat us again!") Nicky Hopkins reportedly opted for touring with Beck that year over Led Zeppelin, even though the Zep were more than willing to pay better. But all concerned or near the action at the time remember almost constant turmoil within the group. On the eve of an American tour in February 1969, Beck, who has by all appearances thrived on or at least made sure to continuously brew up new vistas in turmoil his whole career, fired both Wood and Waller. He told the press that "Their playing had deteriorated." (Hey Jeff, what about the difference between your solos in the versions of "Shapes of Things" by the Yardbirds and on *Truth*?) They were about halfway through cutting *Beck-Ola* at the time—nothing like turning a personal shakeup into a fullscale crisis—and Rod was stunned. The way he saw it, Beck wanted Ronnie out while Hopkins for some reason had it in for Waller. In any case, Rod later said: "Oh dear. Silly boy. He really was. He's really got to go to get another band as good as that."

Overlooking the fact that JUST MAYBE JEFF BECK NEVER REALLY WANTED A FULLTIME LONGTIME "BAND" IN THE FIRST PLACE—I mean, do Segovia or Ted Nugent have them?—one feels duty bound to report that almost identical words were spoken in the winter of 1975 when the Faces were told which bus lines led to the unemployment office, and not by Britt Ekland either.

A month passed in which the degree of merriment and brotherly affections in the

Emergent from psychedelic shadows: blue mods! L. to R.: R. Stewart, bragging in code; Sean Bonniwell, drummer; Ron Wood, younger than he'll ever be; J. Beck, aka "You're lucky I'm here," possibly near death.

Beck camp may be easily imagined. By March 1969 Beck, Stewart and Hopkins were on a transatlantic jet hoping to rescue what they could of their tour, enough of which had by now been cancelled to hurt. They brought along Tony Newman and one Doug Blake to fill in on drums and bass respectively. Blake lasted exactly one show before being fired and replaced by—surprise!—Ron Wood, who rushed right over. It was something to do, maybe not all that different in the final analysis from jumping directly from the Stones to the Faces and back again six years later. You don't have to love somebody to play with them, in fact sometimes true deep hatred brings out the best in all concerned, especially since contrary to eternal myth all rock bands come to hate each other's guts sooner or later anyway so what the hell's the difference? Jeff Beck, that's what. Rod: "By that time, Ronnie was well pissed off and from then on he used the group as a filler while he looked for another band."

From *Creem* January 1972:

GARRY: *I read an interview with Tony Newman where he said that nobody in the band was happy with the way it was going. Is that right?*

STEWART: *Yes it is. The band was together, it was a great band to be in, the music was great, but it was everything that went with it, the aggravations and unfriendliness that developed. It was getting too ridiculous for words, toward the end, when we were trying to escape from each other all the time. One would stay at the Hilton and the others would stay at Hotel Third on the Bill around the corner.*

As Robert Quine so pithily put it: "The only trouble with music is you gotta play it with other people."

Beck-Ola was released with the usual perfect timing: almost the same day the group broke up. With his customary extra dollop of humor, Jeff let it be the first album under his name billed Jeff Beck *Group*. According to Mac Garry, a diligent scholar of these matters, "the album was patchy, to say the least, and it was basically recorded for the US sheep audience—the group was under the impression that a rock 'n' roll revival was about to sweep America and cut the appropriate songs ('Jailhouse Rock' and 'All Shook Up')." Garry interviewed Beck in August '69, as the band was falling to pieces literally all around them: Hopkins had split for California, Ron Wood and the rest of the soon-to-be-Faces were already drawing up plans for world conquest or at least a few thousand nights on the town, and Jeff was busy not bothering to tell Tony Newman he was sacked. According to Garry, Jeff's girlfriend even broke the traditional British Birds' Code of Yardley-Demure Silence by getting on his case about it: "You really ought to tell him, Jeff." "Oh, he'll find out," Jeff reportedly replied.

On the other hand, maybe Newman was relieved, because Beck's next bright idea was to form a Supergroup with Tim Bogart and Carmen Appice. He intended to break up their band, Vanilla Fudge. He didn't tell anybody what he was plotting at first, although he could hardly contain his excitement at the possibilities such a lineup offered: "I nearly fainted on the floor when they phoned me up," he later divulged. Garry: "Beck was totally flabbergasted by the tribute and honor he felt those two cats were paying him."

I guess it's understandable in a way to anybody who's ever heard the Fudge's eight-minute slowed-down version of "The Windmills of Your Mind," but this move did leave everybody else a little confused. From *Creem* again:

GARRY: *The end of the group was a very indecisive affair ... it just fizzled out.*

STEWART: *Yes, we just sort of floated apart really. I was worried about various things like management, the future and Ron Wood had gone, which choked me off because we were getting some nice things together. ... When a group breaks up, the usual line to come out with is 'we couldn't*

74

have gone any further musically.' Well, that's a lot of bollocks. Me and Beck could've played together for years and still come up with nice stuff.

To which I say, *"Still?"* Nobody including Beck liked *Beck-Ola*. *Truth* was mainly notable for the Look-What-a-Flash-Guitar-King-Jeffrey-Is factor—where were all its great original tunes that bands are covering to this day? What whole generation of younger groups did it influence? In my book ''Love Is Blue'' was Beck's crowning masterpiece from that era. It certainly was the ultimate representation of his general attitude toward his audience and his art, even if it was Mickie Most's idea. I'd play it right now if I had a copy! And I bet it'd hold up! Not like *Truth* and *Beck-Ola*, which sound pathetically dated. But then my greatest guitar hero was always Jimmy Reed.

Face it, it was only a pack of cynical Limeys out to be first to cash in on the emergent Superstar syndrome. Carmine Appice admitted as much in a later interview with *New Haven Rock Press*: ''When me and Tim left the Fudge, we were going to get a group together with Jeff Beck and Rod Stewart, but their managers weren't going to go through with it. See, Jeff wanted a group to compete with Led Zeppelin because he was mad at them for taking his thing and popularizing it and taking all the credit. So he was bitter, and wanted to form a group, rather than Beck and his boys, but the managers weren't going to make as much money. Then Beck got in that car crash...''

Ain't rock 'n' roll *glamourous*? And what a great reason for forming a band! Sounds like a bunch of little boys fighting over a Scooter-Pie they shoplifted from the local 7–11. Also this ''his thing'' business—I imagine it might have been news to the other ex-Yardbirds that the entirety of their contribution to rock 'n' roll history boiled down exclusively to Jeff Beck's Thing. Go check the songwriting credits on their albums.

How about ''Beck's Boogie?'' Yeah, that's it, Jeff Beck invented the Boogie. Nobody black in the forties or before that even ever dreamed of such a musical form. I'll tell you what Jeff Beck invented, yet not singlehandedly: the heavy metal guitar solo. His solo on the Yardbirds' ''Mister You're a Better Man Than I'' was THE original primal prototype heavy metal guitar move. Ten million fretbusters since have heard and tried to replicate the chilling fire-and-ice power of it and all failed.

So here we are with Jeff Beck in the process of disbanding his first Supergroup without telling the drummer while breaking up Vanilla Fudge and then hopping a plane to do solo work, leaving everybody totally confused, depressed and screwed career-wise. Actually I admire him for it— everybody else in rock 'n' roll is exactly the same way, except almost none admit it or do it with such style. He's always seemed to have fun at this sort of thing, which makes him far less offensive if not a downright shining example of Humanity at apogee.

Jeff Beck is an anomaly—hell, he may end up the hero of this book, since Ron Wood went and joined the Stones which is cool but kind of like taking a Civil Service job (he sure ain't no freelancer!). And both Rod and Jeff are supreme products of the era from which they first emerged into (not inventive musicianship but) Superstardom. For a prime example of the general mood of the time, what people wanted and got and deserved, let's refer again to Garry/Stewart in *Creem*:

GARRY: *Is it right that the Fudge split up because you wiped them off the stage one night and they just felt they had to give up?*
STEWART: *So they say, yes. We did a gig in New York City which ended up in what they call the 'nine man jam': the stage was full of people including Bonham, Page, Beck, me and Planty, and the guy who used to play bass with Jethro Tull. We were doing 'Jailhouse Rock' and it was fucking incredible. I finished the whole thing*

by shoving a mike stand up John Bonham's arse and he got arrested—the cops pulled him off and I ran away ... We were all pissed out of our heads. And the Vanilla Fudge couldn't follow it, just couldn't and they packed up that night. A few days later, Carmine and Timmy got on the phone to Beck and said they wanted to form a band, keeping me on as well.

Gee, doesn't that just sound like one of the most wildly historic nights in the whole history of rock 'n' roll? Wouldn't you sell every tooth in your mouth just to have been there? Just imagine—all that talent on one stage, and just think how long they must have played that poor old song too. Sounds just like *Animal House!*

Personally I'd rather see the Runaways doing an encore of Lou Reed's "Rock 'n' Roll." I don't find a bunch of exhibitionistic drunks (which people later called the Faces, sneering) singing and playing that hard to come by. There are plenty of Irish bars in my neighborhood where the drunks might not be famous but then again you don't have to pay an arm and a leg to see and hear them.

But don't hold the musicians entirely culpable. Audiences ate this up. By and large they still do. They've read enough interviews, seen enough plugola movies and generally bought the hype (the Biggest Hype, umbrella for all the rest) to the extent they've convinced themselves they're actually enjoying this stuff, it's actually good, means or stands for something, is a special occasion, etc. Man, it was *heavy*—so heavy the poor Vanilla Fudge, who to all appearances were doing just fine until then, had no choice but to break up.

I thought the part of the Fudge's *The Beat Goes On* album where each member of the group in turn got his chance to verbally expound on his philosophy, politics, favorite recipes or whatever while something or other musical played in the background was far heavier and more significant. Certainly better history. But what is history? "Fiction," according to William Burroughs taking dictation from Hassan-i-Sabbah, and they wuz right. In rock 'n' roll ... well, look, almost nobody noticed when Clapton's playing first went cold. A lot of people still haven't. But Dylan, Lou Reed, even Van Morrison—folks (that includes me) can't *wait* to be first to point and jeer: "He's washed up! Burnt out! Nothing left to say!"

Personally and artistically I think Beck was washed up for all time after he was thrown out of the Yardbirds. His ego problems have always been legendary, but the Garry interviews are especially revealing: "Though Stewart admired Beck tremendously as a musician, the group was a disaster socially. Rod admitted that 'In the two and a half years I was with the band, I never once looked him in the eye. I always looked at his shirt or something.'

"I asked him if Beck was as directionless as he seemed—whether Stewart was in fact the pilot.

"ROD: No—I think he gave me as much direction as I gave him. In the early group, Dunbar used to lead if anyone did—most of the ideas came from him—and then towards the end, Tony Newman came up with a lot of ideas—like the original 'Plynth' was his idea, though it was me and Ron's chord sequence."

Just imagine: a Supergroup, led by a Guitar Hero, where most of the best ideas apparently have to come from whoever happens to be drummer at the moment. Somehow it just don't seem right.

In 1971 Rod Stewart still was unlike Jeff Beck in that he could feel bad about criticising his old mate, even if he was only telling the truth as he'd experienced it: "I've said so many nasty things about Beck and yet they're true. But it's very easy to kick someone when he's down, do you know what I mean? But he'll be up again in a

77

couple months—he's got a new band, I offered. No chance. Woody saw him the other night, and you know what? He had the cheek to ask him to join again!''

Though anyone gutsy enough to break up a monolith like Vanilla Fudge just so he and half of them could hopefully make a few million playing what he knew was garbage even though he thought they were better musicians than the likes of Ron Wood ... well, this is not the stuff of ordinary mortals.

Meanwhile, Beck went to Detroit getting everybody all hot and bothered with the promise of some no-bullshitting-around Motown sessions which either never saw the light of day or never happened at all. Depending on who you believe, he either cut with the creme of Motown studio regulars, the guys backing up Stevie Wonder and Marvin Gaye and the Tempts, but the results didn't meet his Olympianly exacting specifications so he nixed release of them; or, according to word of mouth around Motor City, the Motown session guys walked out on Master Beck, because they were used to working with pros instead of prima donnas and, according to *Creem* magazine, didn't even slightly dig ''his pop star airs.''

It was also around that time that he got into a serious automobile accident that put him out of commission for a while. Bogart and Appice joined Cactus and their most memorable songtitle was ''My Lady From South of Detroit.'' Stewart sat down with his old pal Ron Wood and began to make some plans. The October 25th, 1969 issue of English rock weekly *Disc and Music Echo* announced that Beck was recruiting Bogart and Appice, which at the time might charitably be called premature or otherwise plain bilge, and that Stewart and Wood had officially and with serious intent launched a new band called Faces, of which more late-breaking titbits anon.

Folks in the know (or just name-droppers) immediately pounced on this: Aha! *Small* Faces! Fave-rave princes of the Mods, a 48-hour millenarian cult indigenous to early-Sixties Albion whose religion was clothing, their sacred libation amphetamine, existing in violent opposition to a more traditionalist sect known as the Rockers. These two cadres afforded the British media much delight by devoting entire weekends to massing on British beaches and punching each others' faces in. I quote from *Generation X*, a study of the subject by Charles Hamblett and Jave Deverson, published by Fawcett Gold Medal Books in 1964:

''VERMIN,'' SAYS MARGATE J.P.

Sending a whitsun rowdy to a detention centre today, Dr. George Simpson, chairman of Margate magistrates, said: ''It would appear that you did not benefit from yesterday's proceedings. You were part of the dregs of those vermin which infested this town. As such you will go to a detention centre for three months. Take him away.''

London Evening Standard, May 19, 1964

MEAT PRICE AT HIGHEST EVER

Ibid, same front page

Shortly after we read these headlines we talked to John Braden, 18, a London mechanic. He had this to say:

''Yes, I am a Mod and I was at Margate. I'm not ashamed of it—I wasn't the only one. I joined in a few of the fights. It was a laugh, I haven't enjoyed myself so much in a long time. It was great—the beach was like a battlefield. It was like we were taking over the country.

''You want to hit back at all the old geezers who try to tell us what to do.... but they deserve it—they don't think about us, how we might feel.

78

"It was great being in the newspapers—sure, we love reading about ourselves. Who doesn't. Blinkin' film stars and debs delights and social climbers hire publicity men to get their bleedin' names in the papers. We punch our way in, cost-free."

While it is true that they also favored such sonic garbage-cans as the Who, it would seem that the Small Faces were the group of choice among this pack of louts whose numbers were probably highly exaggerated by the dailies in the Stewarts' shop. Though horrible musicians by any standard before Rod entered and taught them all how to play their instruments, the Small Faces did garner some attention with *Ogden's Nut Gone Flake*, a sort of pre-rock opera concept-type album I never bought because it was shaped funny and looked too British for these tastes. Packaged to resemble a to-bacco tin (and *you* know what *other* type of inhalable combustibles that might contain, nudge nudge!), its music was too twee by far. I mean, would *you* buy an album with such songtitles as "Happiness Stan" and "Happydays Toy Town"? The group also had a (very) minor Stateside hit with "Itchycoo Park," which supposedly contained a lyrical reference to some guy smoking marijuana for the first time (you could tell be-cause the track utilized phasing). Its failure was no doubt why singer-journalist James McGuinn, in his *authentic* hit with the Byrds "Eight Miles High," made passing refer-ence to observing, during his first visit to England, *in places/Small Faces hung down*. In shame, doubtless! My own response both to Small Faces and the Mod schtick in gen-eral was like Ringo's answer in *A Hard Day's Night* when posed the Ultimate Ques-tion "Are you a Mod or a Rocker?" He replied: "Neither; I'm a Mocker."

LESTER BANGS

79

From the Faces

to the Faceless: The Peak Years

CHAPTER VI

ON OCTOBER 18, 1969 IT WAS REPORTED IN *N.M.E.* THAT ROD STEWART HAD JOINED the "Small Faces." When Steve Marriott walked out the band had received plenty of offers, but they didn't like any of them. Yet they were determined to stick it out; they knew they had the nucleus of something wonderful, but no immediate clue where to take it. Ian McLagan, who must have been feeling particularly desperate or cynical that week, almost joined Humble Pie, while Ronnie Lane started jamming with Ron Wood, who'd got his teeth into a guitar again and wasn't about to let go. He'd had enough of Jeff Beck's "mercurial" dodgeball for one lifetime, and on the evidence amassed in the years since had apparently while in the latter's employ learned at least one of the most important lessons all but a very few of the greatest R'n'R guitarists have sooner or later come to: that he nor none of his peers warn't no prolixitous Boss Coltranes; nope, his style flew in the face of all that and quickly defined itself till he melted into the igneous jetspews of the Stones.

81

Ron Wood with the Faces sounded like Woodchopper's Ball alternating with swoops and sheets so loose it seemed at first he was merely slinging frets at you. For all the Faces' continually abused and underrated "barband sloppiness," he mastered that particular sluice of custom-channeled Berryblues till by the time of "Stay With Me," it sliced as bone-incisive as any diamond in town. What he mainly knew from the beginning on was what Keith R. first taught us all: that rhythm guitar *is* lead guitar.

Meanwhile Ian McLagan was just about the only major-league R'n'R keyboard man in the whole *decade* who was worth anything, for reasons similar to Wood's ascendance: because he knew Fats Domino wasn't Rudolf Serkin. When the Faces were in full flight onstage he played off his twangtime copilot like a graveyard fulla St. Vitused bones were leaping outta the soil and jangling around each other for sheer joy. This was *it:* a moment that needed no justification unless life itself did, and yes the sick were healed and the dead were raised from Quaalude cement. I know because I was as big a fan as they came.

I am possibly the world's worst audience: I'll sit blankly staring at Leviathan field goaling the parted Red Sea waters, and the Faces actually managed to get *me* on my feet dancing up and down on my shuddering chair as I clapped and whooped like a born-again fool. Beats me how they did it except they never put on airs or artsyfartsied or condescended like Led Zeppelin, who stood there like they were doing us a favor just letting us *look* at their Royal Oglikins.

82

Every Faces show was a party and they presaged one of the real primal meanings of no-bullshit New Wave by letting it be known that we were all in this together so get loose as a buncha jombo squonks sprung from prison and handed a truckload of Jack Daniel's. It seems strange to recall now when every bodycount's so seeming borndead and even stranger if you were young enough to miss it. 'Twas joy un-alloyed *sans* division, even if only for that hour or two. I remember the first time I saw the Faces, at the Santa Monica Civic early in 1970: when they got called back for the encore, they stumbled stage center, slung their arms around each other and Rod said: ''Look, there's just one thing you gotta understand with us: if you ask for one encore, *you're gonna have to take at least five!* Sorry!''

A collective howl of pure love came pouring back, and we all leveled the joint.

Rod knew he looked like a horse with a rooster's ratcombed haystack haircut; Ronnie Lane was a hedgehog who forgot to shave, and too bad; and Kenny Jones did what I wish every other drummer in the world would just do: he sat back there bashing away with a seeming kindergarten mindlessness that was actually the glue holding the band together. If you don't believe me, just guess who was the only Face Rod asked to join that horrendous Backing Band he assembled after shafting these guys in 1975.

But none of them had any idea they were gonna set America and then the world on fire back in '69 when they were floundering around staring at a deaf-mute future. Everything was rotten everywhere, though we all pretended otherwise.

83

Rolling Stone had just begun informing us that the Renaissance of Rock as Quality Music was in full swing, so we'd sit around cringing to things like that Traffic ditty where the idiot squealed: *Uh, wowee, like, uh, geezo weezo—it's jayuzz man!* etc.

Still, the Faces kept faith. They knew the Sixties were over even if nobody else did, which's why I'd just as soon put up with somebody like them clearly marking time on *First Step* rather than suffer the condescension of all those other twerps issuing bloated "masterpieces" because they had to show the world they'd learned a new chord change. It was so depressing that when Wood started bringing his friend Rod Stewart to rehearsals the "Tartan Terror" spent most of the time sitting there staring at them. Later he told John Pidgeon, the Faces' British biographer and post-Rod co-songwriter with McLagan: "I'd listen at the top of the stairs and I thought they sounded good, but there was no one singing. And *they* knew that as well. Ronnie Lane knew that. So it was only a time before they asked me to join."

This brings up the question, never satisfactorily answered, of why, if so much tension later developed in the band because Ronnie Lane felt he wasn't getting to write *or* sing enough, he didn't open his yap and let yawp then and there. I think the answer is that he and all the rest of them always knew he wasn't strong enough to front the kind of world-class band they aspired to be and ultimately became, but nobody wanted to come right out and say it.

One thing I have learned both through observation and personal experience is that the myth of rock 'n' roll bands as four or five happy-go-lucky guys just bouncing through the world is just that: a lie, a cartoon. The Faces when they were really united came as close as if not closer than any other band. The real truth is that most rock 'n' roll bands hate each other's guts. Can you imagine any more perverted Bizarro-world imitation of the nuclear family, after all? There is never a true democracy in rock 'n' roll—it's always either Boss Jock and the Bearers or four or five egos battling it out on shaky ground.

Lane and McLagan knew this in front and held off because they were scared Rod'd end up playing *fuehrer* to the group a la Marriott. On the other hand, nobody else sang like that (tumbleweeds scratching against each other inside an exhaust pipe) or looked like that (Ichabod Crane with nerve enough post-Beck to have forgotten the meaning of shame).

It was a match made from Tinkertoys. Having nothing to lose, they played their first gig at Cambridge University Ball as Quiet Melon. "We went on without any rehearsal and hardly any equipment," McLagan recalled to Pidgeon. "We did 'Hoochie Coochie Man' and 'I Got My Mojo Working' and 'What'd I Say.' It was a case of 'Quick, what key?' 'Doesn't matter—first one to the end's the winner.' "

The Faces' style was already beginning to emerge. They certainly had a unique rehearsal schedule for the time: meet at the pub at noon, get drunk, rehearse a little in the afternoon (the two hours the pubs are all closed by British law, I betcha), then back to the pub to drink their dinner, then rehearse a little more, then close the pubs.

One day they taped a rehearsal and played the cassette for Glyn Johns, who'd already worked with the Small Faces. He took the new lineup into Olympic Studios where in one night they cut six demos that were sufficient to land them a thirty-thousand pound contract from Warner Brothers.

Johns assumed he'd be asked to produce the first album and asked for 2% of royalties accruing therefrom. McLagan dug in his heels and they ended up with no producer unless you counted engineer Martin Birch, a *Beck-Ola* vet.

The album showed it. Producers, for the most part, serve absolutely no purpose beyond gussying up something fresh and alive on demos and running the band over and over the same ground till the whole place is a cemetery. But the most distinctive thing about *First Step* was probably the Mickey Mouse doll they were holding on the cover; they knew they were getting by on being young and English and pretty. Most of the songs were too long, too loose, too jamlike. The album was a grainy *Steamboat Willie* where the film kept breaking; listening to it was like wading through a marsh where the autumnal light on the reeds, and the croaking of the bullfrogs was pleasant but you knew that at least for the time being you were headed nowhere. Stewart was still unsure of himself as a singer, falling back on those trademark "bluesy" falsetto whoops a little too often. The others weren't together: they knew it; everybody was writing songs and none of them were very interesting.

They'd been signed on November 1 with Rod getting "special dispensation" from Mercury to record with the Faces for Warner Brothers, and by February 1970 the album was out. In the intervening year Rod had also cut his first solo album for Mercury, which established him, building on the base first laid by his American appearances with Beck, as a force to be reckoned with in the industry.

The two albums were released the same month and the solo album was greeted by raves equivalent to the bewilderment with which *First Step* was received.

They were swimming upstream anyway, because debuting in the aforementioned Era of Quality Rock they were expected by audiences and industry alike to manifest a certain dignity, decorum, all that boring crap where bands walked out dressed like farmers, plugged in and played with blank faces. This was widely assumed to connote a tastefulness on the part of both musicians and audience. It was of course death, and self-righteous at that.

Whatever else anybody could say about 'em, the Faces were not dead. Gangling idiots was more like it, and from their very first pro gig, where Rod stumbled and broke a bass on his way out of the dressing room, they made their mark as complete clowns. They opened for Taste, Rory Gallagher's power trio whose name in retrospect spoke for itself, at Southhampton Top Rank, and the audience of Guitar Flash devotees were offended not only by their distinct paucity of tasty licks, but their attitude in general. It was pretty much the same story everywhere else they played in Blighty. Rod got himself an aluminum mikestand which he twirled and threw around like a majorette behind enough cognac to stun a moose, and, according to Pidgeon: "The most consistent characteristic of their live performances was a tendency to fall in a heap on the floor in the middle of numbers. Kenny Jones would drum on unperturbed while the others quickly learned to play prone."

At this rate they soon became something close to a national disgrace. Such promising boys. Such wasted talent. The whole nation of England is one big Jewish mother. I'd rather go see five winos than five preening egoes, but other folks seem to have this thing about getting their money's worth by watching somebody pretend to be special when they're not. The complete falsity of this line of reasoning was what ultimately led to New Wave, of course, but at the time a punk was still the buttboy in Wormwood Scrubs and Faces were thought of more as alcoholics than musicians. Rod explained it later: "Nobody wanted to listen to us and nobody was taking us very seriously, and we decided to go round the pub beforehand. Call it Dutch courage if you want, but that's what it was down to. We were just lacking confidence, and I think all the boys enjoyed a drink more than anything else. It wasn't a conscious thing that we wanted to be different from any other band."

They just wanted to be drunks. "There was a general smile whenever anyone played a dodgy note."

Only trouble was nobody else was laughing. As is well known, the British have no sense of humor. Americans, however, are another story. They have a sense of humor but about all the wrong things. They think Frank Zappa is witty and the Jeff Beck Group was High Art. Noting that we were a nation of drunken suckers, and that the Jeff Beck Group had already done far better here than in England, they came on over, and immediate pandemonium set in. Their first U.S. tour, in April and May of 1970, established them as a huge draw; U.S. kids were always restlessly ready for something new. Put it like this: most new British groups—if they were lucky—got to play three weekend nights at the Whisky a Go Go to the *creme* of L.A. trendies. *The Faces played the Santa Monica Civic Auditorium,* your standard huge toilet, and put on the show I was at and described. Part of their magic, of course, was creating an intimate atmosphere in these vast "pleasure" domes that a band would normally enjoy only with an audience in a bar. Bruce Springsteen and ZZ Top are the only other performers I've ever seen pull it off, and Bruce's show is choreographed to the last bead of sweat. Not the Faces. Never.

They also quickly gained a rep for blowing every other band they shared the bill with off the stage. They first did it at their debut "U.S." gig, in Toronto, Canada's Varsity Arena, where they were third billed to Canned Heat and the MC5, no easy trick in the latter's case. The following day, March 26, Lane, McLagan and Jones began to learn what Rod and Wood were familiar with by playing America for the first time. They blew Lee Michaels offstage in Boston and San Francisco, and Savoy Brown in Detroit, which became even more of a Faces stronghold than it had been for the Jeff Beck Group.

After 28 shows they went back to England in June where they played six shows, including one at Dudley Zoo billed below T. Rex, where Edgar Broughton, the worst Captain Beefheart imitation I have ever heard, informed the audience that the Faces were "drunken East End yobbos." October saw them back in America for 28 dates at larger venues than before, where they usually headlined though they never bitched about being second 'cause whoever followed them'd have a hard way to go: Mountain, Eric Burden, Johnny Winter, Three Dog Night, and plenty of others hated their guts. In America at least, the Faces were simply invincible. What had come across as sloppy in Britain was just what the Americans needed desperately.

Things got schizo real quick; one day they'd be finishing off an American tour in the vast Chicago Syndrome, then before they'd even had time to blink they'd be back home, playing places like Wake Arms, Epping, which holds a few hundred. By now Limeys had gotten the point (probably because at that time, in contradistinction to the present, they slavishly followed American trends), and Wood sussed out the difference: "American audiences can *discover* bands, they can break a group, whereas in England they're used to having it set on a plate and reading about it first, the stories getting back to them—in those days anyway. If they read that a band had conquered the States and done all kinds of silly things, then they would be ready for it, but if a band just appeared like it was trying to make a second life out of a name that had been there and gone, it stood very little chance."

Six months after they finished their first U.S. tour they came back, and by the following February, less than a year after debuting over here, they were on their *third*. Meanwhile they'd cut *Long Player*, their second album, and while a definite advance over the first it wasn't all the way there. It was released in March 1971,

Irwin Steinberg, President of Mercury Records, wonders at the strange resemblance between Mr. "Every Picture Tells a Story" and Mark Farner, bustwise, while Rod looks desperately for a backup group.

along with the single "Had Me a Real Good Time" with the otherwise unavailable "Rear Wheel Skid," a derisive tune about Jeff Beck's auto accident, on the flip. *Everybody's* attitude was best summed up by Ed Ward in his *Creem* review: "Well, the Faces took their first step, and, like any first step, it was greeted with reserve. After all, the baby might fall flat on its face with the second step. Here, then, is the second step, and I think we'll have to wait a while before we can categorically state that the baby's learned to walk yet . . . . After playing it numerous times, I find I can still look at the label and not recognize some of the titles. Nor, I find, can I remember what most of the songs sound like." And then, *the very next thing he says is:* "But why deal with the album's shortcomings?"

90

Well, why bother with these babies at all? Jeez, maybe the British were right. Or they were great live and lousy on record, as many people thought. But something was beginning to develop, and it had a lot to do with that Wood guitar signature, which'd initially surfaced on *First Step*'s "Around the Plynth," the original prototype Faces raveup. A concert rouser, sure, but the band was beginning to play with more intensity than they displayed anywhere on *First Step*. What had saved the first LP for its partisans, really, aside from sheer charisma peeking through the dullness, was its very unmistakable Englishness, as if its very obscurity even while spinning on your turntable was somehow evidence of a dense magic only known Over There —if only we'd known! And almost a con, but we enjoyed it and them so much we didn't give a damn. Fittingly (and characteristically) enough, the first album had faded out abruptly in the middle of the song "Three Button Hand Me Down"; no one knew how to resolve it, where it might end up, perhaps really if it should exist at all. Unlike Solo Rod, the Faces had few cover versions to fill in their blank spots and moments of uncertainty.

But Rod was beginning to develop that persona which has brought the Faces glories and mutated grotesquely in his solo career. "Flying" and "Three Button Hand Me Down" were the indications of it on the first Faces album: sheepdog music, and that's no putdown—there was lotsa woof in there, along with the emergent Stewart Song: an Innocent's Progress, with continual references to hearth safety Back Home, and the tension between those roots and the world this naif was stumbling through was the source of the vitality in many of his future opuses.

91

94

On *Long Player*, Rod was playing the Wandering Feckless Minstrel again, a role he was obviously beginning to relish, refine and perhaps most importantly have fun with: "Mother, you won't recognize me now..."

But when he sang "I'm *so* tired," he sounded ironically ready to leap up and move out, as did the whole band. They were just more *alert* (less drunk?), not only going somewhere—even if the destination was still rather vague—but anxious to get there. These early Stewart songs—"Bad 'n' Ruin," "Sweet Lady Mary" and "Had Me a Real Good Time"—were not only about leaving rustic hearthside beginnings and taking a chance on the open road of rock 'n' roll, where Rod was formulating his romanticised picture of the down and out life, but charmingly callow in a way that almost compensated for deficiencies in execution. In other words, if the Jeff Beck Group was a classic exercise in market-conscious Rockstar Cynicism, these two early Faces albums *belied* their own version of a cynicism not so different, after all, with every dropped beat and mushy jam.

Meanwhile, Stewart was quickly learning to write songs that for rock 'n' roll represented a whole new approach to (understanding of) sexual/romantic relationships. *Long Player*'s "Sweet Lady Mary" was a clear precursor to or written (with Wood and Lane) around the same time as "Maggie May," in which the sense that she dropped him was more explicit, and he even admitted he had to "steal away" rather than face her and come to a mutually understood conclusion. Perhaps in this particular universe of women as seen by men, it is only possible to empathize or love when one is such a shambling bumbling tenderfoot that one holds the very concept of Woman in awe—maybe, for Rod or anybody male with this mental set, "manhood," "coming of age" consists of nothing but the "knowledge" that they're not holy Blakean vessels whose flanks are hunks from the very haunch of God, but just a stockyard fulla slags. With the exception of course of the occasional (often/usually monied/famous) Bitch Angel who'll be his at least partial ruination while providing him with grist aplenty for future songs.

But there is something very adult in this song, in that the woman is not at all necessarily the romanticised Whore/grasping aging slattern almost worthy of *Sweet Bird of Youth* he painted in "Maggie May." There is nothing to suggest that this is not a perfectly reasonable, sexually healthy, adult woman growing inevitably bored with a boy still reeling from this experience somewhat beyond his years. Certainly there's nothing here so uncharitable as *The morning sun when it's on your face really shows your age,* or for that matter *You led me away from home/Just to save you from being alone.*

Okay, so the later/other song, the hit, the classic, is more complex in its characterization—it also takes a sly revenge on the woman in the kind of terms that only somebody who looks like Rod Stewart looks onstage today can finally truly appreciate: the inevitable furrowings and saggings of age (small faces were never going to grow old, you see, or so it was oddly enough assumed at the time, and if you want to see something really pathetic take a look at one of the cover pix on *their* "comeback" albums). Maybe he had to recast it that way, but on a certain level, inferior as it is, I prefer "Sweet Lady Mary"—on the level, perhaps, that it's more real. This Coming of Age business is a tricky affair, particularly in rock 'n' roll—once you get there, you're supposedly finished.

For Rod, it had not only begun, the Explosion was just around the corner—in June 1971, just three months after *Long Player* took its "baby steps," "Maggie May" and the *Every Picture Tells a Story* album were released (although "Maggie

May'' almost wasn't the first single from the LP—its flip, Tim Hardin's ''Reason to Believe,'' was the original choice) and both immediately rocketed to Number One on all charts in both America and the U.K., something previously not even achieved by the Beatles. By contrast, *Long Player* had climbed to a respectable Number 29 in America, while neither it nor the ''Had Me a Real Good Time'' single did much in England. In fact, it would be very close on to another year before the Faces started getting hits of their own.

First, though, we've got to backtrack a bit to when Rod was in the Jeff Beck Group and Lou Reizner, then of Mercury Records, saw him perform. Reizner, who ended up co-producing Rod's first two solo albums (something Rod was never too happy with), was a discbiz old-timer: among others, he had or would also produce the Singing Nun, Manfred Mann, Paul Mauriat, Richie Havens, Horst Jankowski, and the horrendous "all-star cast" version of Pete Townshend's *Tommy* in which Rod played the Pinball Wizard, as well as the all-time "all-star" bomb *All This & World War Two*.

So Rod's yapping away with Beck, and Reizner decides he wants to sign him and record a solo album. In a managerial/business war typical of Rod's entire career, Reizner and John Rowlands, the lawyer who along with Geoff Wright was one of Rod's two managers, decided they saw no reason why Rod shouldn't record solo while with Jeff Beck. This was the very beginning of a long series of legal wrangles be-

tween labels and groups which handed Rod, playing the beleaguered innocent Artist, nothing but profit. At the time Beck was managed by Mickie Most and Peter Grant, the latter later of Led Zeppelin, and they thought the idea of Rod Stewart solo albums stank. Rod, they pointed out, was under contract to them, meaning this was money straight outa their pockets, but according to Reizner ''we were able to establish that this wasn't so.'' Rod's contract with Beck only stipulated the two released Epic albums.

This made the Beck Group, who had already been at each other's throats when they weren't stabbing each other in the backs, even more loveydovey. ''Chaos'' would seem the most operable term—everybody wanted to be in a supergroup, THE SUPERGROUP that was going to make it big. Keith Moon came up with the name Led Zeppelin, and it is a fact that he, Beck and Rod gave serious consideration to forming a band with that monicker. There is no other word for this but ''greed'': in June of '68 it had come out that the Beck Group had done record business in the U.S. every bit as lucrative as Jimi Hendrix, The Doors, etc. Yet everybody involved in this scene wanted more. Why?

In Rod's case the answer is simple: he's a miser and a tightwad who apparently trusts no other living human moneywise (not a bad attitude to take in the record biz) although he's perfectly content to fling away fistfulls of the stuff on himself alone and I do mean alone. He says so himself. Here's a random sampling of Rod Stewart quotes on the subject of the relative importance of that green folding stuff in his own life:

''I'm so tight, I don't spend a penny. I don't mind buying a round, but I can't stand buying two.'' (*Melody Maker*, Aug. 25, 1973).

''I enjoy spending money. But I don't waste it. I wouldn't say I'm mean—but there are times when I've got long pockets and short arms.''

''I love the music but I wouldn't be doing it if I wasn't getting paid.'' (*Melody Maker*, Dec. 25—*Christmas, for Christ's sake!*—1971.)

Longtime manager John Rowlands told Rod's British biographer George Tremlett: ''He was always very cautious when it came to money, and I don't think he was prepared to take the risks. Even when he was with the Hoochie Coochie Men, Rod was always well paid, and because his expenses were low and he was living at home with his parents he was never short of cash. So long as he had money coming in regularly and could get up on stage and sing, I don't think he was really very bothered.''

When he first signed with Rowlands and Wright, they discovered quickly that if he didn't see to fiscal sharpshooting (rare among rock 'n' rollers) he'd have somebody else that did. ''Basically, the document we gave Rod to sign was a straightforward management contract. He had the document for about two weeks before he signed it, and during that time he discussed it with his brother who was an accountant—and I think that's why Rod was always so shrewd with his money . . . even in those days he [the brother] was picking up about seventy pounds a week . . . the first time we saw an example of [Rod's] shrewdness was when he said he thought that the contract should not include our getting a percentage of the money he was earning with Long John Baldry because that was something he was already doing before we came along.''

Let's flash forward to Lou Reizner watching the Jeff Beck Group and wanting Rod Stewart on Mercury. Reizner knew Rod wanted to buy a do-it-yourself Marcos car kit, and didn't have the bread, which was a thousand pounds, to do so.

So Reizner gives him the thousand pounds, Rod builds the car, and refuses to record any kinda album for Mercury. A thousand pounds was a hefty chunk of change for signing in 1968 ("practically unheard of," says one source), but Rod didn't think so.

As for the signing of the contract itself, a clause was inserted which stipulated that just in case anybody didn't like the size of their piece of the pie in future, the dispute would be settled according to English law. Mercury agreed to this, and lived to regret it when it caused them to lose Rod to Warner Brothers in a mid-Seventies wrangle between the two companies (who records fulltime for *two record companies,* anyway?), holding up the release of *Smiler* for several months and causing *Coast to Coast/Overtures and Beginners,* the double live Faces album, to be released on Mercury in the U.S. and Warners in the U.K./Europe. You'd think Rod would be content with having been able to have his cake (solo career) and eat it too (Faces) all these years, but no: way he saw it they dehumanized him, and *Smiler*'s release (which occasioned a vast collective yawn anyway and hit the cutout bins in record time) was four months later than originally planned: "Record companies thought they both owned me, which is a very depressing position to be in, because it's like being a bar of soap or a toilet roll or a lamp post."

So Rod signed with Mercury in July 1968, but they didn't get the first solo album even begun until the following July. Reizner: "It all started to become very difficult around June and July, 1969, because now that he'd got his car what Rod really wanted more than anything else was his house. He wanted more money so that he could get this house at Highgate." Then he made his old pal Long John Baldry, who wasn't exactly rolling in dough at the time, pay him *rent* for subletting his old house at Winchmore.

Finally, though, they went in and cut the album. While more together than his primal "Good Morning Little Schoolgirl" sessions, Rod had admitted of *The Rod Stewart Album* (called *An Old Raincoat Won't Ever Let You Down* in England, though Rod wanted to call it *Thin* so bad the word was finally inserted in a way that made it barely decipherable along one side of the cover; to this day absolutely no one knows why): "I didn't know whether I wanted a shit, shave or shampoo, to be honest." So he just cut it with a bunch of his friends, like Martin Quittenton (acoustic git), Woody and Mac, setting a formula that'd stick around for the next few albums: a few originals; a folky type toon or three; equal number covers more or less, usually including one by Dylan; and a sound that differed strikingly from that of the Faces' albums. These records basically were folk-oriented, which was why I always preferred the Faces and doubtless why Rod solo albums always got slobbered over (well, till the late-Seventies) as the Faces albums got slagged: because Folk Music, as everybody knew, was Good Music. Greil Marcus in *Rolling Stone* on *The Rod Stewart Album*: "Imagination pervades the music, in the choice of material, in the frequent use of beautiful bottleneck guitar work to draw out the subtler aspects of many cuts . . . and in the range Stewart himself displays on almost every vocal."

In other words, "tasty licks"! While I will admit that the sound obtained on this and his next few solo albums was unique, it also leaned heavily in the direction of acoustic Ramblin' Jack Elliott doodah, as Rod admitted to *Rolling Stone* at the time: "Folk songs, that's what they are, just folk songs I like . . . 'Man of Constant Sorrow'—a Scottish folk song. That's the one I like best. 'Dirty Old Town' was written during the last general strike in England in 1938 . . . . I used to see these incredible pictures of America when I was a kid. I'd picture Jack Elliott riding his horse across the desert . . . . A Brooklyn cowboy, whew!"

100

A football playing folksinger, whew! All right, I'm being unfair. I'll fess up why aside from simple folkie prejudice I don't like this LP or almost any of Rod's solo work: he's an "interpreter." Of other people's songs. And the first two rules in My Book are: (Number One): "Only one cover version allowed per LP." (Number Two): "No one should ever cover a previously-released rock 'n' roll classic unless the cover is either a radical reworking or actually cuts the original."

The first cut on side one of *The Rod Stewart Album* was called "Street Fighting Man." Rod's version was pointless, pretentious, and even threw in a keyboard vamp from "We Love You" to be cute. He told *Rolling Stone* at the time that he recorded it because he "wanted somebody to hear the words. Such fine lyrics. I wonder why Jagger bothers to write lyrics like that when he sings so you can't understand a word?"

If Rod had read Jagger's interview in *Rolling Stone* scant months before his own, he would have learned that Mick sang that way on purpose and deliberately refused to include lyric sheets with Stones albums because he knew it was more fun getting them a little at a time, picking up new lines every time you played the thing, or even mishearing 'em in ways more appropriate to your own sensibilities. Claimed he learned this from listening to Fats Domino. My favorite line in "Street Fighting Man" is when Mick sings, "Heyyyy, say my name is Gorgeous Gurmus!"

The Stewart folk-based formula for solo albums was now defined, helping set the stage for future Faces-slagging night rallies. As it was, out of nine songs on *Gasoline Alley*, his second solo album released only six months later, only two and a half of its nine songs managed to work their way into live Faces sets: "It's All Over Now" and "Cut Across Shorty" and part of the title cut in Woodrow's slide guitar solo exhibition midset. They had more sense than to ever attempt "Street Fighting Man," about which Rod had lied. He didn't record it because he wanted anybody to hear the *words* (most of his albums with the Faces or solo haven't had lyric sheets —notable exception: *Ooh La La,* on which he refused to write more than a smattering of lyrics). In 1974 Rod finally fessed up to John Pidgeon: "I had an incredible nerve to record 'Street Fighting Man,' because I think the Stones said everything with that particular track that they could possibly have said. But I did it anyway. At the time it was only a filler: we were going to record 'Street Fighting Man' or 'The Girl Can't Help It,' so we went for 'Street Fighting Man' because it had less chords in it."

Rod was lucky. The album got a lot of hype and managed to move 100,000 units in fairly short order in the United States. Which sent Reizner and Mercury President Irwin Steinberg into a quick huddle about getting together another Rod Stewart album while the market was percolatin'. When Reizner mentioned this to Rod, he said: "If you are my manager you have got to get me some more money." Reizner was only Rod's record producer, but he went back to Steinberg, who was amenable as Reizner described it later: "Steinberg said he would give me $12,000 to produce the album, and then whatever part of that I didn't spend Rod could have the difference . . . and it was then that his Scottish ancestry came out and he became very mean and frugal . . . and there were all sorts of scenes in the studio. The cost of producing the LP turned out to be thirty-five hundred pounds"—about seven thousand dollars give or take some loose change in those days—"and Rod kept the difference. Before I finished the album I had to go to the States [for] my brother's wedding and so Rod hadn't had the money. Rod finished the work on the LP while I was over there, and then when I came back he wouldn't give me the tapes . . . he

101

hid the tapes under his bed and he would not give them to me until he got his money . . . . Also he took it as an affront that I had had to go to my brother's wedding, and that I'd put that first before finishing the album . . . we sort of lost touch until he had his hit with 'Maggie May' about 18 months later when we became friends again . . . I used to go out there to see him . . . we got involved again just as he was starting to make money, but he was still one of the meanest guys I have ever known. If you were out for a meal with him he would say, 'I want to buy a bottle of champagne . . .' Then the bottle of Dom Perignon would arrive, and when the bill came he wouldn't reach for it . . .''

Several years later when Reizner mounted his version of *Tommy* featuring

104

Townshend as well as Sandy Denny, Stevie Winwood, Maggie Bell, Richie Havens, John Entwistle, Merry Clayton, Ringo Starr, Richard Harris and Rod as Tommy, Reizner had so much fun he told George Tremlett: "The only problems I had with any of the artists were with him. I chased him long and hard," till finally Reizner recalled that he had once bought and had at great expense restored a certain pre-war Rolls Royce which Rod had been slavering over for years every time he came by the house. So finally Reizner said: "I'll tell you what—I will give you my car as an advance against royalties."

Rod: "I rather hoped you would say that."

Reizner: "I have regretted that ever since. I really loved that car. It was restored to perfection . . . there were always problems with Rod, trying to pin him down to dates. He was the only person I had that sort of trouble with . . . and when we did sessions for his own album, there were problems, too. The guy he brought in as a drummer, Mickey Waller, was the only drummer I ever met who never had a drum kit. We always had to hire a drum kit for the session . . . and then on one session Martin Pugh was going to play acoustic guitar, and I had a guitar that I'd bought— an Aria, a Japanese guitar, which I quite fancied. I took it down to the recording studio and let Rod use it, and then after that I kept asking him to let me have it back, because it really was a good guitar. And then one time I went down to his house at Windsor, and said to him straight out: 'Can I have my guitar back?' And Rod replied, 'Come on, Reizner—that's my favorite guitar!' And he had this room there loaded with guitars."

Gasoline Alley's initial U.S. sales: 350,000. Rod was climbing fast. In fact, the last half of 1971 and parts of 1972 were Rod Stewart and the Faces at pinnacle. That's how it was starting to read on a lot of marquees too: "and the Faces." The Faces had to endure the humiliation of going on Britain's *Top of the Pops* weekly TV show and pretending to play behind Rod while a copy of "Maggie May" whose label bore no other name but his own spun around. They solved this problem by all picking up each others' wrong instruments: Woody sitting behind the keyboards, Kenny Jones on bass, Ronnie Lane behind the drums, etc. But it wasn't enough. It was beginning to hurt. The problem was probably best summed up by George Tremlett: "Curious anomalies. In autumn 1971 Rod Stewart received FIVE Gold Discs for sales in Holland, France, Germany, Scandinavia, and the Benelux countries of *Every Picture Tells a Story*; in the United States it became a multi-million seller; when he went over to the U.S. with the Faces in November even the 20,000 seat Madison Square Garden was sold out two months in advance . . . BEFORE THE FACES THEMSELVES HAD EVER HAD A BRITISH HIT RECORD!"

It was schizophrenia time again. One obvious answer was to work up a hit single (which was just exactly what Stewart and Wood did) and album (much abetted by producer Glyn Johns, who they finally let in the door and thanked publicly on the liner; he certainly did tighten them up), *A Nod is as Good as a Wink . . . To a Blind Horse*.

Dave Marsh, in his review in *Creem*, said the album was about "fun."

From the first strutting notes of "Miss Judy's Farm" you know you're really finally THERE—the band actually sounds *taut*! Lyrics are not only more focused but sexier, and if they betray a certain self-consciousness *re* burgeoning Image, it could only be interpreted (at least that time) as totally healthy, a necessary step. Rod was preening, sure, but you'd have to admit that he was reduced in this song to the role of Supermasculine Menial. If we now had a full-fledged Rock Star on our hands

105

at least he was singing (and convincingly yet) about working in the soil with *his* hands, and was not apathetically buzzing groupies for "Room Service" (an actual Kiss songtitle).

"Stay With Me" was the band's all-time classic, bringing the raveup stratagems from "Plynth" to pinnacle. After this on one level there really was nothing left to do but throw together a few more songs while waiting for the last guest to leave, and then break up.

It's a brilliant song, musical values aside, for how perfectly it articulates a certain frozen moment of sheer reciprocal narcissistic hatred. But all this was *assumed* then. Jolly good hijinx taken for granted. Still is, most places.

Sure lotsa readers've lived this song—whaddaya think, they sit inside refrigerators their whole lives? Well, yes. Together. *Alone* together. The phrase "symbiotic exploitation" floats into view. They/we hate and use each other BECAUSE THEY/WE ARE EXACTLY ALIKE in all respects save one. I wanna make it with you because it's the closest I can come to making it with myself, but I hate myself, so when we're done or before I wake I want you to get your sleazomatic li'l ass OUT of here—unlike Maggie May, the sight of your makeup-smeared face in the morning light might just be too close to the mirror for comfort. Because if I want to penetrate this mirror, then afterwards I want to get as far away from me as possible. Because that person is truly just trash, as he/she has just proven. Leading back once again to my long-nurtured suspicion that narcissism is the beginning of schizophrenia.

But schizophrenia don't make the misogyny any easier to, ah, swallow. It's implicit that he's the rockstar and she's the groupie, so do your duty and beat it. The only thing that could redeem that attitude is the music's force, the song's realism and Rod's sense of humor, which always seems to be turning on its owner even when it isn't. Or used to at least. Unless there was no ambiguity in the first place and even irony was barely left alive, which was probably how it was taken by most folks, who weren't dumb enough by half to overthink every ditty that hits the playlist.

The LP's other masterblister is of course "That's All You Need." Ron Wood sure did know how to throttle up his heebeejeebees back in them days.

One reason *Nod* so far eclipsed its two predecessors (Number 6 on U.S. charts, Number 2 U.K.) was that the first two albums had at least been true *band* records, *i.e.* songwriting credits equally shared by various combinations and permutations within the band plus occasional outside help from the likes of Bob Dylan, Paul McCartney, Big Bill Broonzy, and Public Domain. One thing this means is songwriting royalties for everybody. Another is no bruised egos especially when your "original songs" are just jamming with ad-lib lyrics stolen from dead bluesmen. During those crepuscular days the Faces actually fulfilled the dream that democracy is the way to run a tight rock 'n' roll ship.

However, it's hard enough *playing* with other people on a permanent basis, let alone *writing* with 'em like you all had the same talent quotients. *Ego*, yes, but fax is fax: all successful bands have leaders numbering no more than one (John Fogerty, Ray Davies) or two (Lennon-McCartney, Jagger-Richards).

Here's a clue to the Faces' relatively late-blooming aesthetic success:

FIRST STEP
One song by Rod Stewart and Ronnie Lane

106

One song by Rod Stewart and Ian McLagan
One song by Bob Dylan
One song by Ronnie Lane
Two songs by Ron Wood and Ronnie Lane
One song by Rod Stewart and Ron Wood
One song by Ron Wood
One song by Nobody

LONG PLAYER
One song by Rod Stewart and Ian McLagan
Two songs by Ronnie Lane
Two songs by Ron Wood, Rod Stewart and Ronnie Lane
One song by Paul McCartney
One song by Ron Wood and Ronnie Lane
One song by Big Bill Broonzy
One song Traditional

A NOD IS AS GOOD AS A WINK
Four songs by Ron Wood and Rod Stewart
Two songs by Ronnie Lane
One song by Ian McLagan and Ronnie Lane
One song by Ron Wood, Rod Stewart and Ronnie Lane
One song by Chuck Berry

A Force was developing, as well as resentments. Ron Wood and Rod Stewart wrote together as naturally as they played, which only figured since they'd been best pals. The (Small) Faces did too, but the songwriting Boss had been Steve Marriott, though Ronnie Lane kept his hand in. "Every Picture Tells a Story," "Miss Judy's Farm," "Stay With Me," "Too Bad," "Lost Paraguayos," "Silicone Grown," "Italian Girls," "That's All You Need," "True Blue," "Borstal Boys," "Love Lived Here": all *my* favorite Stewart *or* Faces songs were written solely by Stewart-Wood with the exception of "Borstal Boys" (add McLagan) and "Love Lived Here" (add Lane). Put 'em on one album and you'd have a record that might even make me willing to throw the others out (if you substituted "My Fault" for "Love Lived Here"). And I suspect a lot of other people feel the same way, given the number of hit singles on that list. It wasn't Rod Stewart *or* the Faces that mattered, it was Stewart and Wood all the way. They had met one night in November 1964 when Stewart appeared on *Ready, Steady, Go!* to promote "Schoolgirl," *his first single,* and they ended up going down to Soho to get drunk together. And had only worked together since both joined Beck's crew in early 1967.

They'll probably be friends all their lives, but for sure they were the core of the best songwriting years either one's ever gonna know. The phenomenal success of *Every Picture,* especially "Maggie May" (Stewart-Quittenton), disturbed this chemistry and a hell of a lot else besides. In fact, maybe we can blame the whole thing on "Maggie May," just like the Beatles breakup got blamed on Yoko: if Rod'd got his wish and *really* never seen her face, or written the song with Ron Wood, maybe the Faces including Rod might still be around, trying to look younger than the Stones.

107

In the last half of '71 not only did the unprecedented magical *laissez-faire* alliance of bigtime band and solo superstar actually *work* to the tune of hit albums and singles for both factions, but they did two phenomenally received American tours and *finally* won truly massive acceptance as a live act back home. They blew T. Rex off the stage at the Wembley Festival and played in front of 40,000 people with the Who at Oval cricket ground only two weeks after selling out the Queen Elizabeth Hall.

They owned the world, or that part of it that listened to pop music. In his review of *A Nod* in *Creem* magazine, which was run as a feature article, Dave Marsh handed them the Crown: "What 'Stay With Me' is all about [is that] the idea of establishing a sound for the group is essential: the best AM groups, like the Stones, are identifiable in under ten seconds . . . . In a way, Stewart and the Faces—who have so much in common with Jagger and the Stones—are reversing the process of the Stones' degeneration. The Rolling Stones in their initial incarnation were a band, for which Mick Jagger was the archetype."

The epochal grace of the Faces, *we* thought, was that such a horrible fate as we gleefully imagined for the Stones could never befall them even though they seemed every bit as talented, the Ultimate Rock 'n' Roll Band. It was a nice dream while it lasted. Here's George Tremlett's assessment of Marsh's Utopian ecstacies of egoless Brotherhood: "From the moment he joined them, the Faces lived in Rod Stewart's shadow, because his stage work with Jeff Beck in the States had provided him with an audience waiting to hear his records at a time when no records of his own were being released . . . . And so they started touring the States—often billed as 'Rod Stewart and The Faces'—after making hardly any appearances in Britain.''

In other words, Rod was always The Star, the whole reason for the pandemonium; and them other cats should consider themselves lucky 'cause the way they took America ''by storm'' was a plain *fluke of marketing*. Of course, Tremlett also wrote that when Rod cut his solo albums ''there were moments of tenderness and constant warmth; with The Faces, he would occasionally sound plain raucous'' and ''When . . . Rod Stewart has recorded with the Faces the results have been . . . well, if not disastrous, certainly below the standards one expects of him.''

Tremlett could be dismissed, were it not for the fact that behind all the whoopup *Rod agreed with him* rather than the likes of Marsh, and not just out of ego either. Behind it all, Rod was still a folkie with roots in Al Jolson, and probably, secretly *did* consider this ''plain raucous.''

In the Feb. 12, 1972 issue of *N.M.E.*, Ron Wood worried publicly about his friend: ''Rod's had a lot of problems with success—it totally took him by surprise.''

Two months later, the Faces toured the U.S. with a ''Rock 'n' Roll Circus'' along that included trapeze acts, jugglers, flying motorcycles, etc. *Creem*'s same Dave Marsh wrote a long piece eloquently capturing the band's mood of nervous ambivalence and Rod's inexorable, helpless drift into a remoteness whose shadowy dourness seemed especially weird coming from somebody with the kind of image (plain old reputation) he'd acquired over the preceding years. Here are some excerpts from its summation of Rod's *own* exile on Main Street:

*E*very father needs
*a son and vice
versa: Rod and Billy Gaff.*

LANE: "Generally, to the laymen in the street, we're always going to be Rod's back-up band. But to anyone who takes a little more interest, the truth will be obvious."

MARSH: ". . . The strain is on Rod's face. When he takes a break for a moment, turns his back to the audience and gets a drink, you can see it. It is not a pretty sight—it isn't surliness or anger. Just weariness and tension."

STEWART: "There's too much work . . . . It's draining on the brain all the time . . . writing songs and getting them together . . . There wasn't the pressure there before 'Maggie May' or *Every Picture* that there is now. If they actually want a record by a certain day, I suppose they must have it. That's the drawback—if I could finish the album when I wanted to it'd be all right."

MARSH: "Is it the public?"

ROD: "No, they don't ask me when I'm gonna bring an album out. They just presume. But it's affecting me health. And there isn't any break, because we've got to start working on the group's album when this one's done."

MARSH: "Back at the hotel . . . in the corner, crunched in but removed from everyone, sits Rod Stewart. He is now looking even more dour than usual . . . The rest of the Faces are acting like the chipped monkies they are, bounding in one and two at a time . . . . Back upstairs . . . . Stewart doesn't look like he's having much fun. Aside from the hour or so he spent onstage, he has smiled only once or twice all evening, opened up verbally only when he was given some pictures of himself with David Ruffin."

MARSH NEXT DAY: "Everyone shows up but Rod. We go through all the motions . . . . Central to the discussion is Stewart, who is conspicuously absent."

LANE: "It could've been a problem . . . if it had gotten to Rod's head. It doesn't affect us . . . we all work together any way. There are lots of people askin' us, 'What about...' But it doesn't apply somehow."

MARSH: "Still, it was Rod and the group's management who had made such a big deal of the group being included in all the Stewart stories. Maybe because of his involvement with Jeff Beck, maybe just instinctively, Stewart knows he needs this group.

"He is not equipped for stardom. We talked for a little while later, but he seemed more moody and depressed than any other time I've ever seen him . . . . The rest of the band are sympathetic. Lane offers, 'He probably feels more responsibility if the show's going wrong than, say, I would . . .'

"Rod Stewart [has] that sort of drive that has made him the biggest rock star of the moment, but it's also the kind of thing that is flipping him out."

This is the epitome of the Goodtime Party Band? Well, you know every cliche from every old movie about showbiz and what really goes on backstage. They all turned out to be true. Marsh entitled the article "The Daring Young Man and the Flying Chimpanzees" and Rod's face was on the cover; when one of the Faces first saw it he flew into a rage and ripped the magazine to shreds.

It would have been most fitting if it were Ronnie Lane, who nursed a host of resentments of Rod and the whole situation. Aside from Rod, he had the highest profile in the band purely as a songwriter, yet he was even more the odd-man-out trying to fit his work into this context—a band whose two main writers' sensibilities are 180° removed from all that everybody loves and believes about them, and you can't call them hypocrites. Opportunists maybe; confused for sure.

Lane never belonged in an arena in the first place; he considered them a ripoff.

110

111

During 1972, the Faces joined all the other bands of nowhere-to-go-from-up-here popularity in playing fewer dates in larger venues. Years later he still spoke wistfully of how much he'd missed "lovely gigs in old, shitty theatres with dirty floorboards."

He was also pissed that he didn't get to sing enough, on records or stage, though he acknowledged that his voice wasn't great. About the highest praise for Lane in the entirety of Marsh's "Chimpanzees" article was that "the show is so finely tuned that it even works where once it was weakest: when Stewart hands the vocal mike to Ron Lane," whom Marsh allowed was "a good singer, but he's not Rod and always before it seemed like he was merely giving Rod a break. No more. His songs are good, and his ideas about how to present them are fine. He mocks himself so well you're never sure how serious he is."

112

That's not even damning with faint praise! Before Rod came along, Lane and Wood had what Lane considered a tidy little songwriting partnership. As early as *Long Player* there were definite problems emerging on multiple levels. Discussing that album, Pidgeon wrote: "Lane's themes of love ('Tell Everyone') and homesickness ('Richmond') were curiously out of place in such uncouth surroundings. He was neither willing to submerge his individuality in a group identity nor to channel his creative energies in a single direction: and he was still determined to sing.

"It was Lane who had lost the most by the arrival of Stewart, since the original intention had been that he should handle the band vocals, supported by Wood and McLagan. On *First Step* his singing had been confined to passages of harmony with Stewart, but on *Long Player* he sang 'Richmond' alone, 'On the Beach' with Wood and the opening verse of 'Maybe I'm Amazed' (though in Stewart's favorite key), "something which he would later declare he'd taken as a personal humiliation.

Lane offered his side of the problem to *Rolling Stone*: "What really happened is that I was writing a lot . . . and there was a bit of hemming and hawing when I presented it. I got pissed off in the end because I felt I was contributing a lot more than other factions of the band, to put it bluntly. It was getting very hard to get everyone together. Rod had his career, I think that's what it was. The whole band was built around Rod, and Rod wasn't 100% there. . . . it was good times, but you can't party all the time."

In most of the songs he contributed to the last two Faces studio albums, Lane didn't. I have this theory nobody else seems to share that most of his songs thereabouts are on at least one unhappy level addressed to Rod. How about the following, from *Nod*'s "Last Orders Please," which most critics have described as a love song (which in a very real way it is): *Well, well hello/And how are you?/Fancy seein' you here/Dont' let it show/No no, no one must know/Why they're playin' 'Tracks of My Tears'. . . . But you said you still want me/Oh, you opened up an old wound. . . . Now you've got yours/And I've got mine/And there's no debts or dues/Oh, what can we do?*

DEAR ROD:
It was so considerate of you to pull the rug out from under my feet in such a charming way: nobody else noticed. It's also very nice you could fit all of us in the band into your busy schedule of ascending stardom which after all must proceed like clockwork or Elton John might get there ahead of you. By the way, do even you know where you're really going? Sometimes it seems as though your ego might have swollen to the point that it's finally become your conceit that you really are Sam Cooke or Smokey Robinson. Poor deluded boy. Even you must know that given such delusions neither the band nor our friendship can have any future. But I do retain some vestiges of pride. So you sing your little tunes and whenever there's *room* or *time* I'll sing one of mine, okay? Thank you. I suppose in the end it really is nobody's fault the way things turned out, but right now I'm too bitter to do more than punch your face in. Unfortunately you're an ex-football player and I'm a scrawny little runt, so it's tough shit about that, too.
Fuck off,
RON

That's probably how *I'd* phrase it if I felt sold down the river but chained for the interim nevertheless. We all have our little mannerisms, styles, tics. But I get a strongly similar vibe off Lane's "Debris": *You were sorting through the odds and ends/You were lookin' for a bargain*. Then suddenly we're in the middle of a Management-Labor dispute: *There's more trouble at the depot/With the General Workers' Union/And you said they'd never change a thing/Well, they won't fight and they're not workin'*. But

113

what's this: *Aw, you was my hero/Now you are my good friend/I've been there and back/And I know how far it is/But I left you at the debris/Now we both know you got the money/And I wonder what you woulda done/Without me hangin' around.*

Little guy feels *used*! A clear case of worker/management exploitation with a general strike thrown in. Whatsa matter, dont' it sit well that Rod's bigger'n some o' the Beatles now and you (who used to be hot with the Small Faces) might as well be sitting back in England writing folky li'l woodsy toons and drinking? Then why, when you sing about how once he was your hero, does Rod sing along with you—mixed feelings, eh, wot?

Anyhoo, Rod's next solo album, *Never a Dull Moment*, was appropriately titled, though the band hardly toured in 1972. Released July 21 of that year, it opened with a canard to the effect that Rod had resigned himself to lying back in his humble beginnings like a ole hawg in a bog and cared not a hoot for money, which of course was some hoot in itself. Then there was the one about the jailbait he couldn't (really didn't wanna) take on his Mexican holiday. Then there was "You Wear It Well," perhaps his most sensitive love-song, its sense of *giving* so unalloyed. Then there was the cover, where he slumped dejectedly in an art-deco hotel de paree lobby chair, looking like the poor befuddled wretch he most likely was at that point in his life. He actually *begged the listener's indulgence* in some liner notes, asking them to take the album as it was and not expect it to be an epochal masterpiece like *Every Picture*. So I guess it's not surprising that this was the most Faceslike of Rod solo albums, and as Kenny Jones most prominently among many has pointed out, if he'd put those songs on a Faces album instead . . . but every time "True Blue" came over the car radio you felt glad to be alive.

Not much else happened for Rod or the Faces the rest of the year beyond their first major U.K. tour, the release of an old vocal Rod had done with an obscure Australian group as a session singer, and the release (as a Rod single and without his permission) of "Angel," an all-time in-concert Faces anthem, b/w a version of "What's Made Milwaukee Famous (Has Made a Loser Outa Me)."

The Faces were sinking fast and everybody knew it. It wasn't a question of Rod hoarding the best songs, at least according to Wood: "That may have been going on in *his* head, but I didn't know about it. Songs written with him were with the Faces in mind *or* Rod in mind. We never used to scheme and say, 'Oh, we'll save this one.' "

Trouble was, Rod wasn't writin' *anything* with the Faces in mind any more. The *Ooh La La* sessions were nightmarish by all accounts. McLagan later recalled bitterly to Pidgeon: "Rod wasn't even there for the first two weeks of sessions: we had most of the tracks finished before he even came down to the studio. And when he came he'd say, 'I don't like that,' and he'd be a real downer. It was like being up in front of a teacher—it was very disheartening. All right, some of the tunes were in the wrong key, but how were we supposed to know what key to put them in? We put them in the key they were written in. And when it came down to Rod singing them, either he didn't like the words because he hadn't written any—they were either Ronnie's words or Woody's words—or he didn't like the tune, or he didn't like the key, or he didn't like the way we played it, so it virtually meant that most of the tracks were blown out. 'Ooh La La,' for instance, we recorded about four times, and the first one's still the best track. Rod was supposed to sing it, but didn't like the key and the way we'd done it, so we did it again and he didn't like the words. Then Ronnie Lane tried to sing it, but it wasn't in his key and it didn't suit

123

his voice at the time. Eventually Woody sang it, and I like the way it turned out except I still have memories of how the track was originally—the feel of it. It was a different number altogether really. So the album was a bit forced in a lot of ways: it was hard work and it dragged on and on and on. I don't think it was a *bad* album, but it wasn't as complete as *A Nod is as Good as a Wink*, which was like bang bang bang, whereas *Ooh La La* was bits and pieces.''

I often think that one of the reasons artists of any sort are such bad judges of their own work is that they always will associate the result with the mood they were in at the time, how long it took, how smoothly it went, the state of their lovelives etc. *Ooh La La* made Number One on the English charts and Number 27 on the American, which makes absolutely no sense except as solid proof of what short memories Yanks got: The Faces didn't tour as much the preceding year, so we commenced to forget 'em. But the Faces weren't happy with the album, the critics thought it was blah, and when it was released in mid-April 1973, Rod promptly summoned *Melody Maker* for a cover story interview in which he lambasted *Ooh La La* as ''a bloody mess . . . it was a disgrace.''

He had nothing to be so irate about: ''Cindy Incidentally'' (b/w ''Skewiff (Mend the Fuse),'' a freeform instrumental jam in which the music kept stopping because Wood and Lane were both so drunk they continuously tripped over their guitar cords while Rod bashed the strings inside McLagan's open-lidded grand piano) had made Number One on all single charts in February, and a month later *Disc and Music Echo* published their annual Reader's Poll results in which Rod was voted Top Singer in both the British and World sections. Rod clearly was a fellow with problems. We won't find out what they were from the lyric sheet inside *Ooh La La* because we already know he hardly wrote any of the words . . .

So why is *every song* on side one, the Rockin' Side, co-credited to this old folkie? It's been one of my favorite Stonesy beerblast LP sides since I first got it. In at least one interview Rod bitched about how he had to leave the Faces because they came to the studio drunk and you couldn't even make out the lyrics on the finished tracks, pointing to ''Silicone Grown,'' whose words he was proud to claim as his own because he considered the tune's subject—silicone-injected tits—extremely important and therefore fiendishly difficult to write about. I don't know about you, but I'm not *overly* impressed with a pun about keeping ''a breast of time.'' Didn't stop me from wearing out the cut though. ''My Fault'' was my own anthem as a budding alcoholic clown, and the only line I could ever remember from *it* was ''If I have to fall on my head every night of the week it's gonna be my fault.'' The album, that side anyway, mattered because after all it *was* 1973, year of *Goats Head Soup* and other less memorable slowhands dealt by other bands long forgotten. Looked like Marsh's old *Creem* prophecy might be coming true.

What I didn't recognize at the time was how Lane's dry odes on side two of *Ooh La La* closed the book with a bittersweet resignation. In retrospect, it was doubly ironic for anybody who thought the Faces were gonna supplant those tired old Rolling Stones who wouldn't last out the decade. Like Rod pounding his chest about ''Jo's Lament'' in the dailies when that paternity case happened for real, we had but to pay attention to know: *Thank you kindly for thinking of me/If I'm not smiling I'm just thinking . . . Can you show me a dream?/Can you show me one that's better than mine?/Can you stand it in the cold light of day?/Neither can I, neither can I.*

And that, I think, was Ronnie Lane's adieu to Rod Stewart and the Faces, as they were billed one lifetime too often. You couldn't deny Lane was a man who knew

when to get out: on May 28, 1973, soon as he got home from their most recent tour of the States (a total of seven for him), the bristlychinned little guy who probably finally could not make up his mind whether he wanted to be a blueblood Rock Star officially quit the Faces. He made his last appearances with them on June 1, 3 and 4 at the appropriately named Edmonton Sundown, which was the kind of irony that seemed to follow the band their whole career with Rod.

Lane already had plans for a new group designed to refute the mistakes and what he saw as excesses of the Faces, explaining to *Melody Maker:* "I woke up one morning and thought: "Where's it all going to end?" I'd been at it for eight years, and I still hadn't got around to singing any of me songs. This time last year I went to Ireland, lived in a Land Rover, and went singing in pubs, just so I could sing some of me own songs for a change. I was getting very frustrated. You see, my songs weren't really suitable for the Faces. They are a loud, hard rock 'n' roll band. Whereas this band will be much lighter and looser . . ."

Rustic roll. The twilit mood of *First Step* pressed down home. The critics had already dismissed his *Ooh La La* tunes as "medium-paced, lightly rocking ballads to fill [the LP] out" and "damp squibs, shapeless and dull." Declaring he "cared more for making music than money," he first supported his family via a mobile recording studio he'd had constructed with last big Faces income, and cut a hit single called "How Come" that was acoustic, laid-back, the antithesis of the Faces. This enabled him to form a band called Slim Chance, which was what he'd wanted to name the Faces after they'd dropped the "Small." He tried to take a little "Rock 'n' Roll Circus" show on the road. It was a total financial disaster because backwater audiences figured if anything this different was good it'd be in London instead of out here in Hooterville. They ran out of gas and money in the middle of nowhere and at one point he was down to only one other musician. He was able to release a few LPs and singles, but what kind of rock albums have songs entitled "Only a Bird in a Gilded Cage" and "I'm Gonna Sit Right Down and Write Myself a Letter?" Somehow he scraped together enough money to form another Slim Chance, whose show was described by Pidgeon as "irresistibly exuberant, a cross between a country hoedown and a Saturday night singsong. . . . Whenever he sang, it was hard not to smile with pleasure, harder still not to join in." Pidgeon said his third LP, *One for the Road*, "created something unique in British music: a genuine form of native country music, no capitals, no inverted commas, just music that came *out of the country* and couldn't conceivably be created anywhere else. . . . His compositions reflected the changing moods of country life from the compelling evocation of heat and drought in 'Burnin' Summer' to 'Harvest Home,' which was recorded in a field because 'it felt right that way. . . . ' "

So. While Ronnie Lane was quietly going broke, the Faces were cancelling June '73's European tour because both Kenny Jones and Rod Stewart were suffering from nervous exhaustion and ordered into "complete bedrest" by their doctors, rather difficult to do and audition bass players at the same time. They settled on Tetsu Yamauchi, who McLagan said gave the band "a kick up the arse" but lacked Lane's personality and wrote no songs. There was even less reason for the Faces to be in a recording studio. Lane and Wood wrote and recorded the soundtrack LP for an obscure film called *Mahoney's Last Stand*, a nice little record that lay unreleased till summer 1976, and in July Mercury put out the *Sing It Again Rod* best-of collection. As usual, more was happening where nothing was happening, and nothing was healthier as well. Tetsu debuted on a Summer tour of the Continent and a few

125

(effectively unadvertised) British gigs so they could "sort themselves out," and in August, at the Manchester Hard Rock, Kenny collapsed onstage. An undistinguished Stewart single (Goffin-King's "Oh No Not My Baby") followed, then a short U.S. tour, then a Stewart-penned Faces single "Pool Hall Richard" that wasn't a hit, then nothing till January 1974 when the long-awaited Double Live Faces LP, *Coast to Coast/Overtures and Beginners* was released on Mercury in America and Vertigo/Phonogram in U.K./Europe owing to intra-record company legal hassles. It was reviewed by Charles Schaar Murray in *N.M.E.* thusly: "rock 'n' roll Dean Martin. . .contains some of the sloppiest and most incompetent playing I've ever heard . . . actively painful to listen to. . ." It stiffed out almost unnoticed in this country.

The Faces had become the one thing that, whatever accusations were leveled at them over the years, no one had been able to say before: dull. After giving an interview in which he declared "Now if we all put our heads together and put the Faces first, we'd turn out an amazing album" because "that's what we need: encouragement from within ourselves," Jones released his only solo single "Ready or Not" (written by Jackson Browne) b/w "Woman Trouble" on their manager Billy Gaff's new GM label, which was also releasing some of Lane's material.

No news for most of 1974 either. Sometimes it seems amazing that the Faces stayed together almost a full three years after releasing their last real album.

Not until September did two things happen, and both were indicative of the hopelessness of any attempts at action: within a week of each other, Rod released *Smiler*, his last Mercury LP (save for Xmas best-of repackagings), and Ron Wood unleashed his first solo album which was actually entitled *I've Got My Own Album to Do.*

Smiler was equally astounding in its drabness, an unbelievable (to that date) nadir in Stewart discs. Six days before it hit the stores, he told *Record Mirror*: "Having waited so long to be successful, I found out it was a terrible anticlimax." Critic Greil Marcus called it "rock-star flimsy; accidental genius turned to formula," sales were barely respectable, and in 1976 Rod admitted: "I had me eighteen months of being drunk on success, when I really didn't care too much. And the result was *Smiler*, which is a really shitty album. It sounds terrible to say that because it's like one in the eye for everybody who bought the album, but it's the truth."

Wood was equally frank about the Faces' current status and future prospects in a Sept. 1974 interview: "I guess there was a time when I felt the Faces' music was going stale—but without us really knowing it. Like I never woke up one morning, and said, 'Oh, I'm bored with the band—it was a stage we went through without realizing it. I think Rod got depressed and that's why he let rip in the press."

This was the same Woody who once told *Melody Maker*: "The record companies have always been onto me for years about doing an album, and I've always said 'Aaah, next year . . .' Because I didn't want to get into that high turnover thing of having a solo career and having to follow it through. . . . Rod's been so good at it and he's had so many people tugging at him saying, "Hey, you don't need that band. Come with me and I'll make you Shirley Bassey or Tom Jones . You can do the million dollar a month circuit in Vegas.' If he was that kinda guy he would've walked out."

What had happened to these people?

They'd outlived their *raison d'etre*, individually and collectively, and there was nothing left to do but make money. On September 20 Mercury released a Rod

129

Stewart single called ''Farewell'' co-written with Martin Quittenton and featuring two bonus tracks off *Smiler*. On Oct. 4, Kenny Jones released ''Ready or Not.'' On November 1 Lane was signed to a three year contract with Island records, and released a single called ''What Went Down.'' On Nov. 15 the last Faces single ever was released. It was called (I swear I'm not making this up) ''You Can Make Me Dance, Sing Or Anything (Even Take the Dog For a Walk, Mend a Fuse, Fold Away the Ironing Board, Or Any Other Domestic Shortcomings).'' It was the only thing with any life any of them recorded all year. It got good reviews. It stiffed. On Dec. 23 the Faces set a record for the most successful British tour of 1974, pulling in box office receipts of over 100,000 pounds.

During Feb. and March of 1975 they toured the States again for eight weeks. I was there and rode back from a wonderful, sweaty, wildly rousing show with them in a limousine where the silence was clammy all the way back to the hotel. I interviewed them for *Creem* and couldn't find one quote worth reprinting. The highlight was asking Rod if he ever had to try to *actually seduce* women. He stared at me dully. I don't think he understood the question. On March 5 he met Britt Ekland at a party in Los Angeles.

1975 was the best year for the Faces since 1971–72 summer to summer cycle. The reason was they all hated each others' guts and made it obvious. *Rod* hated everybody in the *band* except *Woody. Everybody* resented the latter because they never

knew if he was planning to join the Rolling Stones. Meanwhile Rod was recording *Atlantic Crossing* without the Faces and turning into an international jetset celebrity. It was wonderful.

KENNY JONES TO *N.M.E.* late–'74/early–75 on the Faces: "I'm in my favorite band. Even if I wasn't in the band, it would be my favorite. We all think like that because we all dig each other so much. And it all comes across on stage . . . we're all basic commoners for a start. And we've been through hard times and been short of money. That's what makes it all worthwhile."

JULY 1975: Kenny Jones claims he hasn't worked for four months due to cancellation of a series of open-air Faces concerts originally scheduled for summer:

''Rod leaving Britain has cost me $500,000, and put the rest of us in a predicament.''

APRIL 1975: One month after Rod and Britt first meet, Ron Wood officially accepts invitation to play with the Stones.

Creem, SEPT. 1976, journalist Tony Stewart mentions a tune on Rod's new album *A Night on the Town,* calling it ''Stones-type boogie'' (''The Balltrap,'' just like ''Hot Legs'' on 1977's *Foot Loose and Fancy Free,* and similar tunes on 1978's *Blondes Have More Fun,* and on 1980's *Foolish Behavior,* which as everyone knows *are* such ''Stones-type boogies'' they're effectively the same song with different lyrics) and Rod explodes in rage: ''But why is it *Stones* boogie music? Why the Stones all the time? Is that the only other band you can compare it to? They're not a yardstick for everybody to measure up against, surely?''

ROD to journalist Barbara Charone, *Rolling Stone,* Jan. 13, 1977: ''If there was one country in the world that didn't love the Faces, it was America. We were always the poor man's Rolling Stones.''

JOHN PIDGEON describing Rod onstage during 1974 British Isles tour: ''When *the band* invited Keith Richard on stage and he overshot his solo, Stewart merely glowered and sliced his finger across his throat. And at the end they all went home in separate cars.''

RON WOOD TO *N.M.E.* on Rod, early Seventies: ''We both bought our first cars together, and our second cars together.''

ROD to *Creem* magazine, Aug. 1975, on Tetsu: ''I've forgotten what he looks like. He's a Japanese chap, isn't he?''

ROD ON RON WOOD to *Creem,* mid–1975: ''Fuck, is he still alive? I really don't know.''

ROD, 1974: ''If Woody was to go, there'd be no point in carrying on. He's a pillar to lean on.''

ROD on his new band, 1976: ''I'd be a fool to go and find a load of drunkards who're going to fall all over the place.''

IAN MCLAGAN on *Atlantic Crossing*: ''It's very sterile, unemotional . . . he wasn't stretching himself. . . . Down deep he hasn't changed at all, but he's into all that Hollywood thing.''

JOURNALIST CAMERON CROWE, ''Rod Stewart Puts on a Happy Face,'' *Rolling Stone,* April 22, 1976: ''LOS ANGELES—Rod Stewart stood on the lawn of his Bel-Air mansion, disgusted and scowling into the afternoon sun. 'I know what you're gonna ask me and I'll tell you the answers right now.' He closed his eyes and recited the newest details of his career, as if for the millionth time. 'My new album is nearly finished. I haven't got a name for it. I haven't got a band and I doubt if I'll be touring again. I don't feel like it. I haven't used anybody from the last album, except for Steve Cropper . . . I used Tom Dowd again as producer because I think he's good. He did a good job on the last one and a better job on this one, especially with the rock 'n' roll. The rock 'n' roll tracks on the last album *A Night on the Town* were useless. Trying to get Muscle Shoals to play rock 'n' roll is useless. That's it.' ''

ROD to Tony Stewart, *Creem* Sept. 1976, on moving to Hollywood: ''When I read those things: 'Oh, Rod's gone to Hollywood and it's spoiled the music and he's no longer hungry' . . . it's such bullshit! I live such a humble life there. You've got no idea.''

132

ROD, same interview, on money: "I haven't been wealthy enough, long enough, for it to spoil what I'm doing."

LOU REIZNER on Rod's latest house, 1975: "I went down to Windsor . . . and they had Tiffany lights hanging down over the dining table . . . it was all very ostentatious. You would ask him how many rooms there were in the house and he'd say, 'I don't really know . . .' And there was a huge entrance hall with a chandelier and black and white tiles, and in the billiards room he had a tartan carpet with all his gold records hanging along the wall . . . you approached the house by driving along a drive that was about half-a-mile long. It was the kind of place where you would expect to find a country squire, and I had the impression that he did not fit into that environment. He seemed a bit lost—although I must admit my car looked good standing outside the house!"

JOHN PIDGEON on Rod's tour, Christmas season 1974: "In Glasgow the Lord Provost gave him the freedom of the city. He beat his chest and spread his arms wide to the audience; 'My people,' he muttered, '*my* people!' "

ROD to Tony Stewart, *Creem*, Sept. 1976: "How can I ever change? I'm working class. I always will be."

Rolling Stone, "Random Notes," July 26, 1979: " 'We're paying a thousand dollars a day for this!' Alana Stewart screamed at several startled minions of the Waldorf Towers in New York, where she and hubby Rod Stewart had just checked into their luxury suite. Touring in style, the couple had decided to seek lodging at the Waldorf—rather than the Hotel Pierre, their usual Big Apple digs—after learning that the Queen always stayed there . . . unfortunately, according to one witness, 'They arrived with two bags and three trunks, and the porters . . . well, one guy was about eighty-three years old—they said, "We've never seen anything like this." So Rod and Alana had to carry their own hand luggage up to their rooms . . .' "

BRITT EKLAND, *True Britt,* on Rod and Mick Jagger: "When Mick and Bianca Jagger dropped in on his trailer to New York before a gig he was distinctly cold and off-hand for no reason. We were all friends and I could not understand his coolness. But later in London, when Rod was appearing at the Olympia, the reason became more transparent. I realized that Rod was actually jealous of Jagger, who still held the throne as the world's No. 1 rock star. Rod's long awaited return to London possibly marked the biggest triumph of his career. Every concert at Olympia was sold out months before and stars and celebrities found themselves in the same position as other fans, having to buy blackmarket tickets from the touts outside the doors. But despite this Rod was plagued by his own insecurity and when Mick Jagger and Keith Richards asked for tickets he deliberately snubbed them. His secretary . . . was instructed to tell them, 'There are no tickets available. We're sorry.' Mick said, 'Okay, then give us a couple of backstage passes and we'll drift in that way.' To my amazement Rod even refused them that request. It was breaking with all pop code ethics . . . he ordered extra security guards at all doors. . . . Tony Toon was speechless . . . I asked him, 'Do you really have anything to fear . . . ?' . . . .Rod ignored my remark. . . ."

ROD to George Tremlett: "I can sing the pants off Mick Jagger."

ROD to Tony Stewart about himself, *ibid.*: "Nothing's changed in me whatsoever!"

In January of 1975, the Faces were back in the studio, cutting tracks. According to Kenny Jones, "It was the first sign of an album being fucking good. For once it had a great deal of excitement in the actual *track*, and the numbers were sounding nice too. All it needed was good vocals and a good mix . . . If we'd continued like that and finished the album instead of going to the States, we'd have made another winner

133

album." Unfortunately, they had to do another American tour, during which they'd booked time in an L.A. studio but didn't get anything done for various reasons having as much to do with the nature of L.A. as anything in the group. After that, though, Jones told Pidgeon: 'I thought we were going to come back and work on the tracks, but instead of that Woody started his album and Rod stayed in the States. So how could we do it? Nobody else wanted to do it. It was all very selfish.''

Pidgeon: "Rod's failure to return home at the end of the tour gave rise to speculation regarding his and the Faces' future. The announcement that he was going to record in America was surprising because it broke a six year old pattern, but his absence from Britain at the start of the fiscal year was more significant, for it suggested that he was planning to spend twelve months in exile from taxation. If he did there'd be no British concerts in 1975 nor any chance of the Faces completing an album unless they joined Stewart abroad. In fact there was no time to record anywhere, because Rod was recording and promoting his LP and Wood was even busier. . . . Before [*Now Look*, his second solo LP] was finished, Ron Wood left for New York where he mixed and mastered it while rehearsing with the Stones for their U.S. tour.''

In February and March the Faces did that U.S. tour of the Silent Limousine, in March Rod met Britt, on April 3 he left England for the U.S. to cut *Atlantic Crossing* and later announced he was going to move here, and in April it was also revealed that Ron Wood would tour with the Stones, but not to worry because the Faces would be touring both America and Britain later on in the year.

The first cut may be the deepest; it's difficult to sort out exactly whodunit. There had been rumors for two years, intensifying when Mick Taylor quit at the end of '74, that Wood was quitting the Faces to join the Stones. They'd always been denied, from Rod telling one interviewer "There's no doubt in my mind that Woody is here for the duration" to Wood himself telling me in an interview the day before they opened their summer–'75 American tour, "It's hardly an idea of any foundation." Still, tour with them he did, from June through August.

I think Ron Wood as a *musician*, at least relatively, *lost* it with the Stones, but not because his playing is wrong. He fits in so wonderfully that it's often hard to tell whether it's him or Keith that's playing, they're alter egos. And he's probably still awed by the sheer fact of being a *Rolling Stone*. (Would *you* wanna be one? Decisions, decisions.) I'm positive he was in 1975, because I saw him with both bands a month apart and the set with the Faces was possibly the best I'd ever seen him play, demoniac yet joyous, while with the Stones he blended like margarine into the general Nothing of that whole tour. I still miss the sight of him in the Faces—four cheery offwhite nubbins bouncing around in back of an amiably fey horse, who pranced and preened and pulled up his baggy silk trousers just like Charlie Chaplin, amazingly enough, just in time to run his bony fingers back through his hair and fling the sweat off with a ballerina bow.

As for *Atlantic Crossing*, at the time much was made of Rod's recording in America; of his using a producer (Tom Dowd) for the first time since Lou Reizner; of how he was coming up with more originals than he ever had since his first solo album; and most of all how he was not using anybody who'd played on his previous solo albums. He went for Memphis/Booker T. boys Steve Cropper, Duck Dunn, and Al Jackson, and Muscle Shoals house band Jimmy Johnson, Barry Beckett, David Hood and Roger Hawkins. He got excited about it: "It's the first time I've recorded without Woody or Mickey Waller. It's a complete change . . . the musicianship is a lot more polished, which is what I wanted, and at last I've found a rhythm section I can really get into."

134

As for the increased songwriting output, Britt Ekland took credit for that in *True Britt*, and I believe her: "As an artist Rod was maturing. I encouraged him to write his own material as I felt he could do much more with his creative talents and Rod was perceptive enough to see the benefits with the promise of larger royalties. . . . he would jot down lyrics on a notepad, occasionally asking me to pair a rhyming word. . . . I used to call Rod my proletarian bard because I saw him as a street urchin writing about simple, everyday things. That part of his life Rod had never left behind and now it was to become part of his poetry. At least Rod was thinking now: thinking and hustling in the same way that I had once seen Lou [Adler, former boyfriend and record company president] involved. Business deals and future projects began to occupy Rod's mind as much as his music."

Some people have blamed Britt for the Rod-Faces breakup in terms so vicious as to become at times downright scatological. This isn't just vile but untrue, with the proviso that what Britt's world *represented* to Rod could only bolster both his ego and his career. I suppose these two clowns loved each other for real, but their romance was *simultaneously* an almost visionary piece of corporate logic on the part of people like Rod's manager Billy Gaff and his publicist Tony Toon: their pairing was like *Grease* and *Urban Cowboy* and *Saturday Night Fever*, those wonderful contemporary phenomena where you use the movie to sell the record and the radio play and record sales to jack up the box-office receipts.

Barbara Charone in *Creem*, mid-'75: "Rod Stewart these days is a changed man. Sitting in his Chicago hotel suite listening to a test pressing of his new album *Atlantic Crossing*, Rod seemed incredibly subdued. That rock 'n' roll flamboyance was now replaced by an eerie smugness. Outrageous conceits no longer decorated his conversation while passionate conviction no longer held up his bold statements. The only time he raised his voice was to put the Faces down."

Then there is the musical factor. Rod has always wanted to be Best Student in Class, and his first few solo albums are A+ efforts, no contest. That's why it was easy for some people to hate him from the beginning: because those albums and the way they were received vs. how the Faces were treated represented a textbook case of the late-'60s/early-'70s idea that rock could somehow be "elevated" into "good music" on a par with jazz, resulting of course in some of the worst and most hideously hubris-corpulent music ever made.

Besides, there's the grand tradition of black American music to aspire to, the records Rod learned most from, by Sam Cooke and Otis Redding and Jackie Wilson and Aretha Franklin. While the Faces are busy turning every arena in the Western hemisphere into a bar, Rod gets it all backwards, decides to ditch the Faces and their provincial Porto-pub forever, and start competing in earnest with his black American mentors (just like he said in that press release back when he cut "Good Morning Little Schoolgirl"). He first-off records with the same cats what backed 'em on all them classic sides cut in these *selfsame* studios. It's the mistake Mick Jagger never quite made, a common one to be sure. Result for Rod was *Atlantic Crossing*, a pallid album that all the Legendary Stardust Sessionboys in the world couldn't prop up.

I asked Ron Wood and Ian McLagan about it just before their Roosevelt Stadium debut in August '75, opining that the ragged but openhearted rightness of the Faces had always been the perfect compliment for Rod's singing and vehicle for his best songs, not that he ever put many of them on Faces albums. "Yeah," said Mac, right after reading an interview in which Rod accused him of practically not being worthy of being called a musician at all, "it's a necessary bit of roughage . . ."

"Actually," said Wood, "the musicians he's used on this album are the cream of musicians. But as far as I can see it's a mistake. It's using people from one kind of musical field and trying to turn them into rock musicians, which they're not . . . Rod's singing tight with a tight band—each track is its own tight vacuum."

"Right," I said. "You hire competent musicians, and you end up with nothing but competence."

"I was asking Steve Cropper," continued Wood, "like, 'Ah, fantastic, you played on 'Red Beans and Rice' and all that, and he said 'I don't remember that.' And he doesn't remember the Sam and Dave things. He remembers some of the songs that he wrote, but there have been so many sessions . . . he just kind of seeks his own genius." Then, reconsidering, he added: "A lot of times it's not a question of being good or bad, it's efficiency. Bear in mind Jackson and Cropper, and respect their approach. Because they invented that little idiosyncrasy in the first place"—in things like "Green Onions" and "Hip-Hug-Her" by Booker T. and the MG's—"and there are plenty of drummers and guitarists who are still trying to get it. We work differently. Kenny just plays the drums the way he would have anyway; and when it comes time to rehearse Rod's old songs with the band I have to learn them all again because I forgot everything. Not exactly efficient, but it's not like sitting up in my room figuring out the chords either, because I play them instantly with the voice. There's nothing to it."

Nothing to it. He played instantly with the voice. Because his guitar and that voice were born for each other, and the most expensive pro in the world is not gonna give you what somebody who loves and knows you will. Anybody knows that. Anybody but Rod Stewart, among a million other egomaniacal artists who make career decisions and cut themselves off forever from their roots, soul, and all-important surrogate family of friends who've been thinking in tandem for so long they can practically read minds. Little Richard said it: He got what he wanted but he lost what he had.

Rod admitted later that Wood and McLagan were right. Two years later, giving interviews to hype *Foot Loose and Fancy Free*, his latest release, he told Richard Cromelin of *Creem* that *Atlantic Crossing* was sterile, and blamed it on his conclusion that "There's no spark at Muscle Shoals, unless you want to turn out disco records . . . they can't play rock 'n' roll."

He threw a lavish press party at a Dublin hotel when the album was released, which only McLagan and Jones from the Faces were formally invited to attend. They didn't show up. Jones again accused Stewart of costing him enormous amounts of money via the outdoor concerts the Faces didn't play that summer. Stewart blamed it on Wood touring with the Stones. Even less surprisingly, when the Faces assembled to rehearse for the tour in Miami in August—the rest of the group was now expected to come to wherever Rod was—there was some doubt whether there would even be a tour. Rod laid it on the line to *Creem*: "If it doesn't work out in rehearsal, then we just won't tour. If it doesn't sound how I want it to sound, that's it. I want it to sound like something new, like the record I've made. We've got to be a lot more disciplined. We've got to tighten up. We always looked at touring like it was party time, which it should be, but it's time we proved ourselves. It's time we took the blinkers off."

On what might as well have been the same day, McLagan told the *Evening Standard* of Aug. 1, '75: "We're going into the studio in November and if Rod isn't

137

going to sing on the numbers we'll do them ourselves. If Rod does decide to leave we'll carry on by ourselves. The pressure is on him to leave at the moment because he's constantly being told he's a Hollywood star and a dedicated leader of fashion. Perhaps he should go solo and try it. Since he's always changing his mind about things, he's going to find it very difficult to be boss unless he's with friends. I hope it won't come to that. I think he still cares about the Faces, but he's up in the air at the moment, being feted by all the people around him. I feel hurt, but realistically I suppose it was bound to happen. Personally I'd just like a bloody phone call or something. At present I get directives through about five different people. He'll say he wants strings on the next tour or he wants us all over for a meeting in Miami. If he wants to act just like that, he will have to hire some musicians on a wage.''

On Aug. 15 the Faces began a 35 city tour of the U.S. in Miami, followed by concerts in Japan, Hawaii, Australia, New Zealand, and then Europe. Rod insisted on bringing along a string section in bowties and tuxedos, as well as a second guitarist in the person of Steve Cropper, to duplicate the *Atlantic Crossing* sound. The band pointed out that this would cost a lot of money from which none of the rest of them would benefit, since it was promoting sales of *his* album, and they could get a string synthesizer for McLagan to play which could create an almost identical orchestral effect. Rod got his way, though Wood put his foot down about Cropper, and got Jesse Ed Davis instead. During the tour, Rod was a distant figure, his name billed above the band's everywhere, sticking to his personal publicist Tony Toon and Britt Ekland. By now the two were turning up in gossip magazines/columns, glossy rags and dailies everywhere.

The tour was a spectacular success, and the concert at Roosevelt Stadium in New Jersey was the best I had ever seen them play, which was saying something. The string section creaked and groaned, miserably out of tune, but the whole band and particularly Rod and Wood were downright brutal, Wood chopping his guitar savagely as if to say: ''*This* is what you're throwing away, you son of a bitch!'' Dave Hickey, reviewing the show in the *Village Voice*, wrote: ''The Faces, throughout their career, have always been defined by the very tenuous nature of their existence. They have never been transformed from blokes into musicians . . . If the Faces ever really achieved stability, they wouldn't be the Faces any more. And if Stewart ever becomes a full-time solo artist, he will be less of a performer and personality than he is today.''

It was such a grand success, in fact, that by September Rod was telling *Melody Maker*: ''At first, it seemed like we would break up. But we're playing better, it sounds tighter. I'll be honest . . . I think we'll stay together.''

KENNY JONES: ''He just likes to confuse the press.''
JOHN PIDGEON: ''When the tour wound up on November 1 no one thought they were saying goodbye for keeps, but sometime later Stewart and the band just melted apart at opposite ends of long-distance telephone lines.''

On Dec. 19, 1975, it was reported that Rod Stewart was quitting the Faces group. For keeps, for good, forget 'em, the end. He blamed it on Ron Wood. While in the official announcement Rod would only say that ''I have only just made up my mind. But I'm definitely quitting this time,'' Tony Toon announced: ''Rod feels he can no longer work in a situation where the group's lead guitarist Rod Wood seems to be permanently 'on loan' to the Rolling Stones.'' Billy Gaff, Rod's manager said: ''Rod thinks the world of Ron Wood. I have repeatedly tried

138

to telephone Ron, who is touring with the Rolling Stones. I have left messages for him to call me, but I've heard nothing.''

IAN McLAGAN: ''I won't believe he is leaving the Faces until I hear it from his own lips.''

KENNY JONES: ''If this means the end of the Faces, I'm not bothered. I expect I will survive.''

On the same day as Rod's organization's announcement, Mick Jagger said to the *Evening Standard*: ''Nothing conclusive has been arrived at . . .concerning . . .Ron Wood joining the Stones,'' although he admitted that Wood had been recording with them in Munich and Montreux . Paul Wasserman, the *Stones'* ''publicity chief,'' told *Rolling Stone*'s Tom Nolan a month later: ''Rod Stewart has been talking about leaving the Faces for three years.'' Rod added later: ''It was such an unprofessional band. I mean, how many times can you get away with being an hour and a half late at a gig for 15,000?''

RON WOOD: ''I didn't want to believe it at all. I thought surely he must be interested in the group, because they're the ones that have to live together, have to sit through those boring hotel rooms and everything; but evidently I was wrong. I was willing to sit through anything until we got to the final thing that we were after, which we never reached. That was the only thing that annoyed me, that was why I was willing to do an album *and* make it good, even if Rod wasn't going to be on it—make it the best-structured of the lot. But in a way that wasn't meant to be . . It wasn't until Rod made that drastic decision that it was obvious I had only one path.''

KENNY JONES: ''He wanted to join the Stones, it was obvious. And it was obvious that he liked everybody and didn't have enough guts to turn round and say it in the first place—'I want to join the Stones'—to everybody. Because I think if he'd done that in the first place, when we were all there . . . the band would probably still have been together with another guitarist. Woody always plays both ends against the middle, so he doesn't lose, and it's about time everybody woke up and saw that. I'm not defending Rod at all, I'm just saying that it's not *all* Rod.''

But Wood's exit was the last straw for the Faces, beyond a doubt. Without Rod, they started planning to cut a new album, the first in three years, and Tetsu and *aide de camp*/roadie Chuck Magee even flew to France to shop for studios, while everybody set aside time after the first of the year and worked on new material. Warner Brothers gave them the go-ahead, then changed their minds, saying the band would have to guarantee they'd tour to promote the album once it was made. Pidgeon: ''Wood couldn't or wouldn't make promises, so there was no money upfront to cover studio costs. And no longer any reason for the Faces to exist. In January of 1976 it was all over.''

It was not until 1977 that Rod finally admitted, or claimed, that it was his decision alone to break the group up. ''We would still probably have been together, just drifting on and on and on if I hadn't put my foot down and said, that's it!'' he told Tony Stewart of *Creem*. And to *Rolling Stone* he was even more blunt: ''The Faces breakup had nothing to do with Woody playing with the Stones. Ian McLagan and I couldn't get on any longer. Mac and I hate each other's guts.''

Ian McLagan to *Melody Maker* on the possibility of Rod or Ron Wood leaving the band, April 1974: ''It's just a standing joke. Maybe someday it'll backfire on somebody, I dunno.''

LESTER BANGS

139

Rod: RIAA Certified Casanova

CHAPTER VII

MANY OF OUR READERS HAVE DOUBTLESS WONDERED WHEN WE WERE GOING TO GET *around to dealing with Rod's rep as a great lover. Can he really be all that good? Is it just a lot of showbiz hype? The answers are yes and no. Some people have even imputed that Rod's some kind of closet queen. What rubbish! He's just a fun-lovin' guy who boogies out in L.A. in his three million dollar mansion in the most exclusive section of Brentwood having nothing but parties which are so much FUN FUN FUN to attend they've become legendary. Rod has been described more than once as the "Perle Mesta of the Strip," which he cruises nightly in Lou Reizner's Rolls Royce Silver Cloud with smoked windows so he can see OUT at YOU but YOU can't see IN at him–ALTHOUGH if you happen to be eighteen years of age, leggy, stylishly dressed, wearing spike heels and flaming red glossy lipstick, and oh I almost forgot to mention FEMALE, and what's most important and absolutely essential HAVE BLONDE HAIR GROWING OUT OF YOUR HEAD, Rod will be more than happy to take you home with him and let his little dogie git along, after which he will serenade you with "You're in My Heart," about what a stuck-up wickdip his ex-girlfriend Britt Ekland is. In said pop classic he lets the world know that she got abysmal taste: try to stick up things like Aubrey Beardsley prints all over the walls of Rod's palace a desecration right there cause this ain't no damn Barnard dorm.*

141

BRITT'S AND ROD'S romance has been well-documented, especially in 1980, when Britt startled the literary community with *True Britt*. Said tome was hailed as "One of the truly great biographies of our time, a fully-accomplished work of modern experimental writing and incisive socioeconomic commentary on Hollywood's current modes of 'corporate' moviemaking, including journalistically nonpareil close-up portraits of some of the most popular faces and names *and* most powerful men in the industry—the only way to explain its impact might be to imagine a cross between Dylan's *Tarantula*, *The Autobiography of Malcolm X*, and Bob Thomas' bio of Columbia mogul Harry Cohn, *King Cohn*." So said *The New York Times*, and no one was surprised when the book won Britt a Pulitzer Prize as well as the National Book Award. Especially after her experiences with Rod, who really seemed to prefer her in a domestic role as he continued to play the peroxide field. All this acclaim certainly enabled her to hold her head high once more as a truly contemporary artist.

True Britt's section on her breakup with Rod documents *her* season in Hell, pouring a torrent of poetic anguish unmatched since Arthur Rimbaud himself, whose "First Delirium: The Foolish Virgin/The Infernal Bridegroom" sounds from title alone like Rod 'n' Britt's situation.

Let's compare Rimbaud's and Britt's poetic styles and see what literary and sociological conclusions we can draw:

ARTHUR:

> Let us hear the confession of an old friend in Hell:
>
> "O Lord, O Celestial Bridegroom, do not turn thy face from the confession of the most pitiful of thy handmaidens. I am lost. I'm drunk. I'm impure. What a life!
>
> "Pardon, Lord in Heaven, pardon! . . . All these tears! And all the tears to come later on, I hope!
>
> "Later on, I will meet the Celestial Bridegroom! I was born to be *His* slave.—That other one can beat me now!
>
> "Right now, it's the end of the world! Oh, girls . . . my friends . . . no, not my friends . . . I've never gone through *anything* like this; delirium, torments, anything . . . It's so silly!"

BRITT:

> I broke down and cried. I felt hurt, cheated, betrayed. Our whole future together, our hopes, our dreams, were shattered . . .
> In my diary I unfolded my anguish . . . "My own private earthquake". . . "Lies and deception" . . . "Snakepit" . . . "Hell not far away". . . and "Alone at home with a hole through my heart."
> My love and respect for Rod crumbled, like parched earth beneath the feet. There was nothing left, except for a burnt-out shell.

Obviously these two pitiful wretches writhed in the throes of distinctly similar plights, at least when they composed these outstanding blue yodels.

Right now, though, you're probably asking yourself: "Just what kind of man could turn his woman into Arthur Rimbaud?" One who called her "Poopy," that's what, as Britt reveals in one of the less elegiac sections of her masterpiece, where she also reveals his brand of love talk. While making a film called *Slavers* on location in Rhodesia, she entreated him to cable a few sweet nothings her way: "I said to him, 'Why don't you send me a romantic message? I miss you so much out here.'

"The romantic message came by return on Telex. It said, 'Dear Britt. Here is the romantic message you wanted. Tired of wanking. Please come, Soddy.'

"Soddy was my pet name for Rod. There were times when he was such a sod even in his most charming moods. Rod coined a similar term of endearment for me. He would call me Poop or Poopy, which had all sorts of unsavoury connotations but as far as I was concerned he meant it in his most affectionate sense." Not like when she put henna in her hair and he commented: "Mind someone doesn't mistake you for a carrot."

They first met at the London charity premiere of *Tommy* produced by Lou Adler, her boyfriend before Rod came into her life. Her first impression: "With his

mousey-colored cactus-spiked hair, an elongated, mobile face and his limp figure swathed in yards of tartan, he resembled a rag doll."

This won her heart almost immediately, and Rod was similarly impressed. At a later party at Joni Mitchell's house, he actually turned down the chance to jam with Bob Dylan just so he could talk to her. "From that moment," she avers, "we were inseparable. . . . Very soon we were making love three or four times a day. We were like two pieces of interlocking jigsaw and we matched physically. We were both slender, small boned and long legged.

"Members of Rod's band said he usually fancied big boobed amazons. I was hardly that, and I asked Rod, 'Do you want me to have a boob job', thinking he must be dissatisfied with my miniature equipment."

But no. Rod was more than satisfied: "Rod regarded every orgasm as a testimony of his love for me. Greater love has no man!"

143

*The Celestial Bridegroom &
handmaiden: "She Bonnie, me
Clyde." (Yeah, but who does the
car belong to?)*

In fact, he loved her so much he wanted their affair broadcast to the rest of the world via "Rod's personal publicist, a lackey with the tongue-twisting name of Tony Toon [who] would indulge in the slickest and cheapest of gimmicks in order to gain his client as much space as possible in the British press.

"Rod would only have to burp and we would cry out, 'Why isn't that on the front page, Tony?' . . . My alliance with Rod was Heaven-sent as far as Tony was concerned. We were the 'hottest' couple in the world, in terms of news-media exposure, and Tony glorified in us, describing us as the 'Burton and Taylor' of the 'seventies.

"I found myself almost echoing Tony's publicity blurbs and playing on the Burton and Taylor theme. What I lacked in diamonds—and it became transparently obvious that Rod wasn't going to give me any—I compensated for by wearing the gaudiest of costumes to match those of my new pop hero."

And that was going some, as Dave Marsh attested in his review of a 1977 Stewart concert in *Rolling Stone*: "He comes on in heavy pancake makeup, wearing skin-tight glad rags that expose his right nipple, and he prances more prissily than ever." Then there was the time they took a holiday cruise aboard the Queen Elizabeth II, and Britt described her noble swain: "At nights, after dinner, he walked the decks in his red silk lined black velvet cape, reliving in his mind the whole *Titanic* disaster. He would even claim to hear 'voices' as he leaned over the ship's rail." But all vacations must come to an end, and knowing how expensive that one must have been it's a small wonder that "There were areas in which I actually saved him money by waiving the services of a valet and make-up girl when he was on tour.

"I would spend hours darning and mending his stage costumes, mutilated by his footlight gyrations and more especially by fans . . . I would also make him up both on tour and in private life.

"I would pencil a thin black line around his nugget-brown eyes and dab in matching brown shadow above the eyes which I would highlight with mascara. The process was more elaborate for his stage appearances, and then I would add rouge and sealing powder. Ultimately he would resemble a marionette."

Given all this, is it any wonder that Rod referred respectively to Lou Adler as

147

"the Rabbi," and former husband Peter Sellers as "That *old* man of yours"? Britt: "Then he would preen, 'Aren't you lucky to have someone at last who is so young and gorgeous?' "

She certainly was. She could have lost out to any one of his countless past loves, including actress Joanna Lumley, of whom Rod said after their first date: "It was the cheapest night I have had out for some time. The meal was £8.90. I thought to myself, 'There's a nice girl . . .' " (Lumley: "I love him to death!") Or model Kathy Simmonds, one of Rod's first blondes, of whom Rod said "We are a little bit in love," also admitting at the time that it was seeing Marilyn Monroe in *Gentlemen Prefer Blondes* that had given him such a thing for them: "I've never stopped dating them," he told the *Daily Express*. "I've lost count how many." Or Dee Harrington, who waited patiently for him in London all the while he was rumored to be involved with President Gerald Ford's daughter Susan, although Dee did admit to the *Daily Mail* that "We have some violent rows. Once I threw a milk bottle across the kitchen at him but he can retaliate, too. How? I don't like to say . . . well, he has hit me."

Yes, Britt was indeed a lucky girl, although Rod told Tony Stewart of *Creem*, "She's a silly bitch." Britt broke in: "But it's very easy when you're in love and you've met someone and everything is fantastic . . ." Rod: "Shut up, Britt! Why don't you shut up? Let the *men* get on with the interview."

The end for Rod and Britt was as dramatic as their meeting. She ran into her old beau George Hamilton at a wild party at Allan *Grease* Carr's digs, with George's

148

Britt wasn't having any of this malarkey, however: "It was my belief that we should share everything together. Our lives, our emotions, our belongings and our futures."

Then a miracle! Rod and Liz *finis*! "I can never leave you, Poopy," swore Rod. But soon the papers were full of Rod with this starlet, Rod with that, so Britt, who was filming *The Great Wallendas*, found herself falling into a new romance with "Bubba, a twenty-two-year-old American boy who was a high wire artist."

"In Bubba," she writes, "I found a fresh will to live."

Meanwhile Billy Gaff said Rod was willing to settle out of court for $200,000. But Britt stood her ground: "I knew my lawyers were seeking $12,500,000. They could not have been asking for an amount like that without reasonable grounds.

"But I wasn't interested in the money." All she really cared about was Rod. So he came back yet again! Bye Bubba! Unfortunately, Rod also had a habit of turning up at night drunk with the boys in his backing band, and with what Britt referred to as one "floosie" after another. "Even when he stayed home Rod acted in a strange, unrecognizable way . . .

"I was looking like a ghost . . . I could not think or act rationally . . . I even began to snort cocaine, from the very packages I had warned Rod about . . . I had a total nervous breakdown. [I was urged] to change psychiatrists and I consulted Aaron Stern . . . The fees were $100 per session and I went every day for a whole month but my sanity was worth it."

Things were brightening till Bianca Jagger called and asked for Rod. She wanted to know when he was coming to Spain. That was the last straw. She telephoned Lou Adler to rescue her. He loaned her a thousand bucks and sent her to Hawaii.

As for Rod, he ended up marrying Alana Hamilton in the spring of 1979, and they even have a baby girl. Their prospects look bright indeed. But then, whose don't?

LESTER BANGS

151

"Everyone Has His Reasons"

CHAPTER VIII

SIX YEARS AGO, WHEN I WAS ASKED TO SUM UP ROD STEWART'S CAREER FOR *The Rolling Stone Illustrated History of Rock & Roll*, I'm afraid I responded by assigning both the artist and his first six records—*The Rod Stewart Album, Gasoline Alley, Every Picture Tells a Story, Never a Dull Moment, Smiler* and *Atlantic Crossing*—to a rock & roll heaven so unbelievably pure that even a saint (let alone a good-hearted, semirepentent sinner) might feel unworthy of walking around the place.

Since 1975, there have been four more LPs—*A Night on the Town, Foot Loose & Fancy Free, Blondes Have More Fun* and *Foolish Behaviour*—not all of them bad by any means. But, from the vantage point of 1981, the Stewart story certainly turned out differently from what most of us expected in 1975. As a young man in his twenties, Rod Stewart seemed to possess an age-old wisdom: some of the things he told us we could have learned from our grandfathers. In his thirties, however, he suddenly metamorphosed into Jayne Mansfield. What was a fan to think? Because of its instantaneous, com-

bustible and life-affirming/life-threatening nature, rock & roll—not unlike first love—often changes so fast that you don't know what to make of it. Hoping you're not a total fool, you close your eyes, kiss the girl, and she shows you the door. But is it an entrance or an exit?

Smiler and *Atlantic Crossing* should have been the tip-offs, I suppose, yet they didn't sound like such terrible turning points then. Perhaps we were still blinded by the beauty of *Gasoline Alley* and *Every Picture Tells a Story*, or by the singer's genuinely likable personality. (Hard to believe, but Stewart was considered the Bruce Springsteen of his time: our least-affected, most-down-to-earth rock star.)

Anyway, I'd like to reprint a few paragraphs of my six-year-old valentine as just that: a heart, carved in a tree by the side of the road with many forks, several of which I didn't see. Let some of the legend linger, I'd argue, because parts of it are still true. Maybe, with Rod Stewart, the past is all that lasts.

These are the paragraphs in question:

> To a lot of people, Rod Stewart onstage in midstrut—blond hair flying, handy with brandy and partial to the broad smile and easy wink—offers as good a definition of the full flash of rock & roll as we're likely to get. He's a wizard at the spotlight game, his long legs quickly laying claim to the private turf of a public master. Behind him, the Faces, the group that provided B-movie backup throughout most of his concert career, careen like well-oiled parts of a perpetual-motion machine gone somewhat daft of purpose, while their leader lines out antics and anthems, holding everything together with the soft-shoe strength and near-total accessibility of his talent and personality. Mick Jagger, Roger Daltrey and even Elton John—the last a pumped-up Dr. T.J. Eckleburg on Sunset Boulevard to Stewart's alley-scuffling, eyeballing Gatsby—may excite some audiences as much, but the Rolling Stones and the Who are formal institutions: visceral, more precise, a little threatening and definitely less friendly. Stewart, even in front of tens of thousands, projects an ex-athlete's warmth, sets up towel-snapping camaraderie among the players, and somehow manages to embody both the extrovert, one-of-the-boys hijinks of the macho carouser and the introvert, aw-she'd-probably-never-notice-me-anyway self-consciousness of the shyest kid on the block. Even as we envy his outgoing, big-winner's style, we revel in the knowledge he provides via self-mockery that he can lose as often and as badly as we do.
>
> This swashbuckling Britisher is a bravado specialist who conversely displays a lucid vulnerability as if it were the sharpest, chip-on-the-shoulder belligerence. Langdon Winner has written of him: "The music of Rod Stewart helps us to remember many of the small but extremely important experiences of life which our civilization inclines us to forget. . . . He can recall these fragile moments of insight to our minds without destroying their essence. As I listened to *Gasoline Alley* . . . I found myself saying again and again, 'He *can't* understand *that*.' But he does." A rock & roll private investigator, Stewart could have sprung full-blown from the pages of *Black Mask* as one of those likable, melodramatic professionals who, born on the dark side of the tracks, now traverses the neon streets of fabulous dream worlds with nothing more (and nothing less) than a head filled with the memories of hard experience and a heart full of innocent mush. Even his present-tense, picaresque adventure stories seldom stray far from the melancholy air of sweet remembrance which permeates virtually all of his fatalistic tales of tender but inevitably lost love. To quote film critic Manny Farber, the best Stewart songs "travel like a shamus who knows his city" well and who respects his own raspy, idiosyncratic ability to locate and itemize small niches within larger ones. Once he's arrived at the heart of the matter, Rod Stewart has an uncanny technical flair for establishing the mood of a song at the outset and sustaining that mood until the last listener is convinced. Some of the primary traits of his complex and contradictory persona are those of the thriller hero and romantic pseudogangster who live life lavishly, sampling the finest wines and loveliest women without ever becoming jaded or having to pick up a heavy physical or psychic tab. Doubtless, Stewart could always use his mellifluous charm and grace to circumvent the sterner issues, but brains rather than brawn seems to prevail. In the end, his ferocious brassiness is generally undone by straightforward, heartfelt

common sense. Essentially, his art conforms to the same strict moral and aesthetic guidelines set down by the mythopoeic American pulp genres— Appalachian folk music, skiffle, folk-rock, rock & roll, R&B—from which it grew and to which it constantly refers. Like Philip Marlowe, he is as sentimental as the Beatles—but much tougher. Like Sam Spade, he is fully capable of falling in love, then, because of some higher artistic morality, sending over the loved one in the final reel (e.g., his leaving the Jeff Beck Group after two LPs, the Faces after five). Whatever his reasons, he's preferred to do his solo albums—by far his most important work—with handpicked musicians who (except for long-term friends Ron Wood and Mick Waller) usually weren't boys from those lusty, often lusterless bands of which he was once a member.

Throughout his career, Stewart has maintained equal and enviable reputations both as a superb songwriter and as a skillfull interpreter of material other than his own. On *The Rod Stewart Album*, the artist undoubtedly functions more impressively in the latter role, but on his best records—*Gasoline Alley, Every Picture Tells a Story, Never a Dull Moment*—the pendulum swings decisively in the other direction. While Stewart's interpretive powers never diminish, several of his own compositions clearly represent the high points of an entire career. Whether he's reveling in luminous licentiousness to the incendiary beat of knockabout rock & roll ("Every Picture Tells a Story," "Lost Paraguayos,") or sadly reflecting upon some lost woman to the evocative accompaniment of rustic fiddle or ringing mandolin ("Lady Day," "Jo's Lament," "Maggie May," "Mandolin Wind," "You Wear It Well," "Still Love You"), he's always believable, and his plight often sympathetic. Stewart's musical flexibility within the low-budgeted voluptuousness of his characteristic filigreed sound is astonishing yet understandable given his moralistic preoccupation with a past which ties tenderized but old-fashioned guilt to a prodigal son's AC/DC desire to return to his more conservative roots ("Don't you think I better get myself back home?") and to flee at all costs the newfangled commitments of the present and future, ("Tearing down the highway in the pouring rain/ Escaping from my wedding day"). In such a philosophical predicament, the singer can lament, "It's been so long since I had a good time," while idly contemplating a dose of "Dixie Toot" hedonism that he knows won't provide any real help. Indeed, Stewart's hell-raising sexist would probably be harder to take if he weren't so honest ("Cause I ain't forgetting that you were once mine/That I blew it without even trying"), susceptible ("Now I'm not so young and I'm so afraid/To sleep alone for the rest of my days") and self-deprecating ("Think of me and try not to laugh"). His compassionate love songs scan like the second thoughts of an unsteady protagonist who "get[s] scared when [he] remember[s] too much" because it's central to his nature to nearly always waver in the face of meaningful choice. "True Blue" starts out as an expression of pure anguish ("Just don't know what to do") but ends with the exhilarating roar of the hero's Lamborghini as he drives blithely away from all of his problems, while "Italian Girls" reverses the process, metamorphosing from happy-go-lucky carnality into a delirious day of reckoning when the stunned Stewart realizes that leaving the woman was exactly what he didn't want to do. From "Gasoline Alley" to "Down in the alley again" in "Stone Cold Sober," the artist exhibits great humanity but little permanent change. With his shy-guy verities and slapstick-exuberant male truths intact, he remains the consummate introspective rock & roll romantic. Like all good romantics, he unwittingly destroys everything he touches. Only to feel damned sorry about it later.

The same concerns are only somewhat less apparent when Stewart pursues his more restful role as an interpreter. If he had never written a word of his own, he would still deserve a place in the history of popular music for his almost unerring choice of material, the canniness of his production concepts and the scope of his emotional range as a singer —arguably the finest in rock & roll. Consider the evidence: "Man of Constant Sorrow," "Only a Hobo," "(I Know) I'm Losing You," "Tomorrow Is Such a Long Time," "Reason to Believe," "Mama You've Been on My Mind," "I'd Rather Go Blind," "Jealous Guy," "Sailing" and especially "Handbags & Gladrags," "It's All Over Now," "Country Comforts," "Angel," "Twisting the Night Away" and "Drift Away." In "Drift Away," he darkens the mood to catch perfectly the poignant persona of a young man who feels he may have missed something essential in his daredevil ventures and now needs a place to hide out while he reconsiders and reaccepts his shrinking options. To me, Dobie Gray's hit version of a few years ago sounds routine and unemotional when compared with Stewart's striving desperation. When this North Londoner sings, ''Oh, give me the beat, boys, to soothe my soul/I want to get lost in your rock and roll,'' he seems to mean it. I can't think of another artist who so fully exemplifies Jean Renoir's iridescent and unforgettable credo: ''You see, in this world there is one awful thing, and that is that everyone has his reasons.'' Rod Stewart understands this and makes us understand it, too. I care about him. In the end, quite a lot.

WHEN *ROLLING STONE* updated its *Illustrated History of Rock & Roll* in 1980, I didn't have the heart to expand the Stewart chapter. There'd been so little I'd liked of the new work, and I'd changed my mind about some of the old. Each time I saw the man, we seemed to have less and less in common. I really hated his Hollywood, male-tart/starlet image, the manner in which he responded to (and completely misunderstood) punk rock, and the way he blamed the press—instead of himself—for turning his early fans against him.

This is what Greil Marcus had to say in 1980:

> Rarely has a singer had as full and unique a talent as Rod Stewart; rarely has anyone betrayed his talent so completely. Once the most compassionate presence in music, he has become a bilious self-parody—and sells more records than ever. A writer who offered profound lyricism and fabulous self-deprecating humor, teller of tall tales and honest heartbreaker, he had an unmatched eye for the tiny details around which lives turn, shatter and reform—the way a lover tears up drafts of a letter, the way a boy combs his hair in the mirror, the way a man in trouble looks for solace—and a voice to make those details indelible. Adopting the persona of a 19th-century Montana homesteader waiting out a bad winter with his wife, of an old man watching his granddaughter squander his savings, of a young man hellbent to nowhere but finding love anyway, he removed all doubts: this is real, you said, this is how it is. Then, full of the rewards he received for his work, and seemingly without noticing, he exchanged passion for sentiment, the romance of sex for a tease, a reach for mysteries with tawdry posturing, and was last seen parading his riches, his fame and his smugness, a sort of hip Engelbert Humperdinck, a rock and roll Porifio Rubirosa. Perhaps it makes sense. When Rod Stewart was learning the game, Simon Frith has said, the goal of show business was not to become a great artist, but to spend money and fuck movie stars. If it was necessary to become a great artist in order to get the money to spend and the stars to fuck, well, Rod was willing. . . .
>
> *Smiler* was just rock-star flimsy: accidental genius turned to formula. Stewart broke up the Faces, replaced his band with expensive American sessionmen, and, within a year, had left England for tax exile. In 1976 he was denounced by the rising punk rockers as the epitome of the corrupt star living off the gullibility of his audience, blowing his fans a kiss while his heart held only contempt. He provided no reason to make one think the punks were wrong.
>
> There have been more albums since—huge hits, some of them, pandering, sleazy records, the humor forced, the compassion just a gesture, the sexiness burned down to everyone else's open shirt and stuffed crotch. Stewart bought himself a band—hacks incapable of playing a note that had not already been bled dry. Stewart seemed comfortable with them; they couldn't push him, because they wouldn't understand the idea. He couldn't push them, even if he wanted to; they'd fall down.
>
> And yet there is one exception, the hit single from the otherwise flaccid *A Night on the Town.* That is ''Tonight's the Night,'' a seduction song so transparent, helpless, and forthright that not even a cynic —which is what Stewart has made this fan—can resist it. The tune glows; you root for the singer, put yourself in his place, in the place of the woman he's singing to. It's not even an echo of his old music—it's new. And then it's over.

SO HOW DO the ten LPs rank now? Like this, I'd say:

The Rod Stewart Album   C +   *Gasoline Alley*   A

Every Picture Tells a Story	A +	*A Night on the Town*	B
Never a Dull Moment	A–	*Foot Loose & Fancy Free*	B–
Smiler	D–	*Blondes Have More Fun*	D
Atlantic Crossing	C	*Foolish Behaviour*	C–

PAUL NELSON

157

EPILOGUE

Rod vs. the Punks:
A Duel to the Death; Or, Before You, My Dear Gaston

TO BE ENGLISH IS TO BE CONSCIOUS OF TWO THINGS: (1) YOU USED TO RULE THE world, and (2) All your current rock 'n' roll bands stink, but the liberal or Left-leaning fan is obliged to like them even though they all sound either like old tarpaulins being dropped in a well while a sickly whelp mewls piteously; or they sound like seven college students hoping for at least a C + even though they are dashing off a project entitled "Twitch of the Miscreant" in between beerbusts.

I ask you, is this any way to conduct a social system, much less a rock 'n' roll scene?

The reason you will probably find yourself strongarmed into sitting through whole LP sides of these ghastly sonics, equivalent to the air in Greyhound bus stations, is that all of these "bands" are politically correct. None of them are Nazis. Many, in fact, have read the first three chapters of *Capital*. Influenced by a certain sentence therein which they misinterpreted due to convoluted mental workings which accompany amphetamine-assisted 3 A.M. cramming for finals, they have seen it as their duty to do away with Imperialism. The "dialectical materialistic" lyrics on their albums are rendered intentionally indecipherable because, owing to the nature of the music itself, they feel it only behooving to mix it in such a way that the whole thing sounds suffused by a blanket of exceedingly heavy smog.

The only people in the world who care about these groups, of which there are hundreds in Britain, are: England's weekly *New Musical Express*; six American rock critics writing for the most prestigious papers in the country to an audience of capitalist Pepsi-swillers; and Rod Stewart. He hates these bands with a livid passion, because he is terrified that they know something he doesn't and consequently may someday supplant his position of seemingly unassailable hegemony at the very top of the *Billboard* charts. He has never heard of any of them (no one including the members of the groups themselves listens to their records, except certain rock critics in aforesaid American journals and *New Musical Express*, the latter only playing them once so they can figure out something to say in reviews which invariably hail the albums as masterpieces, after which they sell the discs for drug money), so quite naturally his paranoia rages even more brushfire rampant than it would otherwise; he dwells on them till they take on indescribably grotesque dimensions. Rod is after all an

158

unusually imaginative man, and frequently he has nightmares brought on by these obsessive mullings. As often as two or three nights in a single week he has awakened with a start which finds his clammy sweatcaked body lunging out of bed like a snapping mainspring, the effect of which occurrence on the lissome Alana Hamilton sleeping beside him one may well imagine.

''Again?'' she cries, real tears every time. ''O my Conqueror . . .'' (for that is her pet name for him suggested by the great man himself).

''Shut yer hole,'' Rod invariably replies, whereupon Alana promptly falls back to sleep, proud in the knowledge that Rod speaks the language of the *torero* when addressing the ladies, which of course is one reason he is so popular with them and internationally pined after.

Then he gets up, goes into the kitchen and drinks a quart and a half of Remy Martin as fast as he can, after which he calls up either Elton John or Gary Glitter, rousing them from 3 A.M. previously peaceful slumber to rant incoherently cross the wires till dawn. They put up with it because neither of their careers is exactly on the upswing, and they are both hoping that he may yet work some record industry magic on their behalves which will eventuate in their becoming even bigger stars than he is, after which both plan to never speak to him again as long as they live and report all his most embarrassing private weaknesses, thus eventuating in not only the ruination of his career and rep as a Great Lover but will finally make him the laughingstock of the world, after which he will be totally forgotten and any sliver of celebrityhood for him a thing of the distant past.

Inasmuch as the sales of *Foolish Behavior* were below Warner Brothers expectations these events may well come to pass. If so, the remainder of Rod's life will find him on a barstool in a shabby section of London, soaking up cheap hootch and telling the same stories about his days of fame and glory over and over again to the other barflies who all agree he is the most annoying wino they have ever met. This will continue for decades, till one night a drunken sailor on leave will stab him in the ribs fourteen times after telling him to shut up about Britt (or ''Whatever her bloody name was'') for five straight hours. He will be deposited in the city morgue, an ''Anonymous'' cadaver, and buried in an unmarked grave.

We know that this tale has not been a pleasant one, but present it in the hopes that readers considering careers in the music industry, at least those who nurse dreams of becoming rock stars, will mark its tragedy and in honest pragmatism reconsider their options, perhaps going into accounting instead. Bookkeeping for record companies, on the other hand, should not be thought at all perilous as career decisions go, and indeed could very likely prove far more lucrative than previously suspected.

And what of all the would-be political bands mentioned at the beginning of this passage, you ask? By that time one and all will be teaching school themselves, where they will get their just comeuppance for however inadvertently murdering Rod by suffering each semester through ''conceptual'' pranks and plain sadisms even more heinous than their own were. Except for one of them. A former member of a band called Essential Logic will be Prime Minister, and go down in later history texts as the most ineffectual and congenitally befuddled occupant of that post in the history of the Empire, which by that time will have shrunk to a territory ranging from London to Stoke-on-Trent and thirty miles either way in the other two directions, the rest of the nation having been annexed by Belgium and turned into an internment camp for children.

LESTER BANGS

159